CHILDREN OF THE HEALER

The Story of Dr. Bob's Kids

Bob Smith and Sue Smith Windows
As Told to P. Christine Brewer

Parkside Publishing Corporation
205 West Touhy Avenue
Park Ridge, Illinois 60068

Smith, Bob, and Windows, Sue Smith, as told to P. Christine Brewer
Children of the Healer

ISBN 0-942421-48-5

Printed in the United States of America

10 9 8 7 6 5 4 3 2 1

Library of Congress Catalog Card Number: 92-64114

"We don't receive wisdom;
we must discover it for ourselves after a
journey that no one can take for us or spare us."

—Marcel Proust

TABLE OF CONTENTS

FOREWORD

Only two people are still alive from the time when Bill Wilson came to Akron and, with Dr. Bob Smith, founded Alcoholics Anonymous (A.A.). They are Sue Smith Windows, who still lives in Akron, and Bob Smith, who now lives in Texas. As they tell their stories for the first time, they give eyewitness accounts of the birth of Twelve Step recovery.

By recording life inside the house at 855 Ardmore Avenue in 1935 and beyond, Sue and Bob paint a powerful picture of how one person's recovery is not that of the family, and how each family member must find the answers for him- or herself. The struggles and founding of Alcoholics Anonymous in their home provide the backdrop.

Sue and Bob requested that their stories be told in the first person, just as their father's and others' are told in the Big Book of A.A. Thus, their stories are presented without analysis or psychological interpretation.

NOTE ON ANONYMITY

In keeping with the Eleventh Tradition of Alcoholics Anonymous (A.A.) which preserves an individual's anonymity, no last names are mentioned in this book. Initials are used. The only exceptions are Bill Wilson and Dr. Bob Smith, the co-founders of A.A., whose identities are a matter of public record.

DEDICATION

There are those personalities in our lives who remain a blessing to us and our families. We gratefully dedicate this book to our parents, Dr. Bob and Anne, for their eternal sharing of experience, strength, and hope.

Bob Smith
Sue Smith Windows
June 1992

For the loving God who allowed me to lead a very exciting life and also loved me through all of my many mistakes and who allows me to be of service and to make amends for some of the selfish things that I have done. For the constant love and understanding of four good kids and a steadfast wife. I am truly grateful.

For my loving parents who tried to instill in me values to sustain me by their tireless example. For the many friends I have met and know as a result of Twelve Step programs. You have taught me a way of life in these programs that I never would have figured out by myself. I am truly grateful.

Bob Smith
June 1992

THE TWELVE STEPS

1. We admitted we were powerless over alcohol—that our lives had become unmanageable.

2. Came to believe that a Power greater than ourselves could restore us to sanity.

3. Made a decision to turn our will and our lives over to the care of God *as we understood Him.*

4. Made a searching and fearless moral inventory of ourselves.

5. Admitted to God, to ourselves, and to another human being the exact nature of our wrongs.

6. Were entirely ready to have God remove all these defects of character.

7. Humbly asked Him to remove our shortcomings.

8. Made a list of all persons we had harmed, and became willing to make amends to them all.

9. Made direct amends to such people wherever possible, except when to do so would injure them or others.

10. Continued to take personal inventory and when we were wrong promptly admitted it.

11. Sought through prayer and meditation to improve our conscious contact with God *as we understood Him*, praying only for knowledge of His will for us and the power to carry that out.

12. Having had a spiritual awakening as the result of these steps, we tried to carry this message to alcoholics, and to practice these principles in all our affairs.

INTRODUCTION

At any time of the day or night, a meeting of Alcoholics Anonymous could be taking place anywhere in 118 countries, attended by any one of 1.5 million people who are active in the A.A. fellowship today. The big, blue book on the table at every meeting is *Alcoholics Anonymous*, the "Big Book" which sets forth the principles of A.A. It has sold more than 7 million copies in the U.S. and Canada, and unknown numbers in other countries. It is published in 14 languages.

Alcoholics Anonymous was founded by two alcoholics, Dr. Robert Holbrook Smith and William Griffith Wilson, known thereafter as Dr. Bob and Bill W. Together, the Midwestern doctor and the flat-broke stockbroker found a way to arrest alcoholism, a progressive disease for which there is no known cure. Their method works, and it doesn't cost anything. Not only does their method work for alcoholism, it also works for many other types of addictions and behavioral disorders. In fact, it has been so successful in changing behavior and keeping it changed that it has been adopted by many groups of people who for one reason or another need to learn how to live all over again. So, not only is there a Gamblers Anonymous and an Overeaters Anonymous, there is also a Families Anonymous and an Incest Survivors Anonymous.

The foundation of Alcoholics Anonymous and other similar programs is the Twelve Steps. The Twelve Steps were developed over a period of four years by Dr. Bob and Bill Wilson and were published in the Big Book for the first time in 1939. Although Bill Wilson wrote the steps, they are an articulation of the program he and Dr. Bob had developed together with Anne Smith, Dr. Bob's wife, beginning in 1935. A series of unlikely coincidences brought together in Akron the three people in the world whose combined ideas and experiences catalyzed to create the A.A. program.

Dr. Bob was born in St. Johnsbury, Vermont, August 8, 1879. He was the son of a judge and an overprotective mother. His wife Anne would later blame his mother's rigidity and formal religiosity for his drinking. Although Anne would eventually learn not to blame anyone or anything for the disease of alcoholism, she would still maintain that Dr. Bob's youthful excesses were in defiance of his mother's rigid control.

Dr. Bob was a popular young man, well liked for his cheerful willingness to thumb his nose at authority. He did well enough in school and entered Dartmouth in 1898. In spite of heavy drinking, he graduated in 1902. After a few unsuccessful years of conforming to his mother's wishes that he enter the business world, he entered the University of Michigan as a premedical student in 1905. He was 26 years old. His alcoholism progressed, resulting in his being forced to leave in 1907. He finished his M.D. at Rush University in Chicago in 1910 when he was 31. He interned at City Hospital in Akron, Ohio.

In 1915 he married Anne Ripley, after what he would later call their "whirlwind courtship" of 17 years. Their son, Robert Ripley Smith, was born in 1918. Unable to have more children, they adopted Suzanne Smith in 1923. She was the same age as their son.

Dr. Bob suffered the inevitable progression of the disease in spite of his best efforts to stop it. He tried many cures and voluntarily hospitalized himself on several occasions. Nothing worked.

In 1933 Anne Smith began attending Oxford Group meetings with her friend Henrietta Seiberling. The Oxford Group had been brought to Akron by a wealthy founder of the rubber industry because the group appeared to have sobered up his son. Unfortunately, the son relapsed, but the Oxford Group stayed.

The Oxford Group had been started in 1921 by Frank Buchman, a Lutheran minister from Pennsylvania. After a spiritual experience while traveling in Scotland, he began a movement to restore first century Christianity to the modern world. Oxford Groupers wanted to change the world by changing people, and they used what they believed to be early Christian methods to do it. Their "five procedures" were later adapted for some of the Twelve Steps: (1) Surrender to God, (2) Listen to God's guidance, (3) Check the guidance with other members, (4) Make restitution to those you have harmed, (5) After careful self-examination, confess your defects to others, either as a witness to change or as a confession to alleviate guilt.

An important part of the Oxford Groups' appeal was their fellowship. Their reliance on home meetings where enthusiastic followers extended a friendly hand to newcomers later became the basic structure of A.A. Other qualities that were transposed into A.A. were their insistence on keeping the program at a personal, simple level, avoiding abstract, analytical discussion, and their emphasis on the positive, joyous appeal of a "changed life."

Oxford Groupers were encouraged to keep attending their individual churches and to use the Group as an adjunct to their spiritual growth. By avoiding identification with any particular denomination, they could appeal to all except Catholics, who were prohibited from engaging in the group's open confessions.

The appeal to Anne Smith was immediate. She gained the fellowship of the group, found spiritual kinship, and saw in it the possibility for change in her husband. She convinced Dr. Bob to go, and he found himself attracted to the group by what he described as the "poise, health and happiness" of its members. He wanted what they had, so he became a regular at the Wednesday night meetings for two and one-half years.

In the beginning, he was reluctant to "confess" to his alcoholism. When he couldn't stop drinking, Henrietta Seiberling received "guidance" to have a special meeting for him where everyone would confess to something "costly" and thereby encourage him to confess his alcoholism. It worked. He openly confessed to being a "secret drinker," everyone fervently prayed for him, and he got drunk again. Dr. Bob did everything the group advised, yet he still got drunk. Something was missing. It was Bill Wilson, another alcoholic.

At the same time that Dr. Bob was pursuing change through the Oxford Group, Bill Wilson was attending Oxford Group meetings in New York. He had been introduced to it by his friend Ebby T., a miraculously recovered drunk, who, upon investigation, had decided there might be an alternative to the death sentence of alcoholism.

Bill had arrived at the Oxford Group by a route as circuitous as Dr. Bob's. He was born in East Dorset, Vermont, on November 26, 1895. Deserted by her husband when Bill was 10 years old, his determined, intelligent mother left him in the care of his maternal grandparents while she pursued a career as an osteopathic physician in Boston. Bill spent the remainder of his childhood in the town of Rutland, Vermont. He began his secondary education in the fall of 1909 at Burr and Burton Academy, where he experienced the death of his first love, Bertha Banford. In the following years he entered the army, began drinking alcoholically, married Lois Burnham in 1917, served a stint in World War I in France, pursued dreams of wealth and grandeur on Wall Street in the '20s, and during the early '30s sank ever deeper into his alcoholic abyss. During 1933 and 1934 he entered Charles B. Towns Hospital four times where he encountered Dr. William D. Silkworth, who was the first person to tell him that alcoholism was an illness. This information didn't appear to help in his recovery, however.

One day in November 1934, his old friend Ebby T. came to see him. Bill noticed right away that Ebby was a changed man. For one thing, Ebby was dry. Not only was he dry, he was enjoying it. Ebby explained that he had found a new way of life with the Oxford Group, and he convinced Bill to go. Bill went to the Old Calvary Church group in New York and liked what he saw so much that he celebrated by drinking. But after that, he managed to stay dry, and he enthusiastically tried to bring the cure to other drunks, without success.

In 1935, when he met Dr. Bob, Bill's career on Wall Street was on its last legs. He was broke, and he and Lois were only able to hang onto their house on Clinton Street by virtue of her small salary. As Dr. Bob's son Smitty likes to point out, at that time Lois was the only one in either family who was reliably employed. When he got a chance to make some money by representing a client at a proxy fight in Akron, a newly-sober Bill jumped on the first train. He lost the proxy fight and was left stranded by his associates in the Mayflower Hotel with the desolation of failure and a growing urge to drink. Faced with the open doors to the bar in the Mayflower, he decided his only hope was to find someone to talk to in an Oxford Group. On the Saturday before Mother's Day, he called an Episcopalian minister, Dr. Walter Tunks, a long-time Oxford Group enthusiast who was to surface repeatedly in the lives of the Smiths. Dr. Tunks referred him to Norman Sheppard, who in turn referred him to Henrietta Seiberling. Henrietta told him to come right over, as she had just the person for him to meet.

The next day, Dr. Bob went to the gatehouse on the Seiberling estate where Henrietta lived, and the historic meeting between him and Bill W. took place. It was Mother's Day, May 11, 1935. The two men had been looking for the same thing and were talking the same language. Bill supplied the critical element that Bob had missed in two and one-half years of Oxford Group meetings—one drunk talking to another. This was the key to it all. Bob immediately grasped the importance of service in the maintenance of sobriety.

Henrietta arranged for Bill to stay at the Portage Country Club for two weeks and then he came to live with the Smiths at Anne's invitation. Shortly afterward, Dr. Bob went to a medical convention in Atlantic City and came back drunk. Bill and Anne sobered him up and got him ready for an operation he was scheduled to perform on June 10. On the morning of June 10, 1935, Dr. Bob took his last drink, a beer given to him by Bill to steady his hands before he performed surgery. On that day Alcoholics Anonymous was born, at 855 Ardmore Avenue in Akron, Ohio.

The two men knew they had to help other drunks if they were to stay sober themselves. Bill decided to stay for the summer so they could work together. They began a vigorous campaign to find and treat other drunks. There followed a long, hot summer of enthusiastic recruiting and fearless experimentation. As Dr. Bob's son recalls, "Those early ones had a rugged time."

The first one, Eddie R., was a failure because of underlying mental illness that only presented itself when he dried out. The next one, Bill D., was a success. A succession of others followed, with varying degrees of success and failure.

The two men didn't have a program. They were groping their way toward one, putting together an eclectic amalgam of Carl Jung, the Oxford

Group, biblical sources, Wilson's spiritual experience, Anne Smith's practical applications of spiritual principles, Dr. Bob's personal and medical experience of alcoholism, and many other diverse influences.

Doctor Bob began going to Akron City Hospital and later, in 1939, St. Thomas Hospital to identify prospects and dry them out. He required that every new "pigeon" spend some time in the hospital, partly because detox was a necessary prerequisite to any intelligible conversation, and partly to emphasize that they were indeed suffering from an illness. Dr. Bob developed a lifelong friendship with Sister Ignatia of St. Thomas, who is still remembered today as a sort of A.A. saint.

Slowly, Bill and Bob developed a little group of recovering people who formally met at Oxford Group meetings but kept in constant communication with each other at get-togethers in their homes. The Smith's house on Ardmore Avenue was the hub of the Akron group, and the Wilson's house on Clinton Street was open to the growing New York fellowship.

In 1938, Bob and Bill began accumulating stories for a book. Bill decided that they needed something to promote what they were doing, and a book would do it. It would explain everything and have personal testimonials to back it up. Many of the personal stories were written at Dr. Bob's dining room table. They were all compiled for the book, and Bill wrote the chapters describing the program. At that point, he articulated the Twelve Steps, the first written description of what he and Bob had been doing. He asked Anne Smith to write the chapter on the family, since she had actively organized the families into a support system of their own. She was too self-effacing to do it, so Bill wrote it himself. *Alcoholics Anonymous* was published in June 1939. Sales were disappointingly slow.

With the publication of the book, the alcoholics, who had for some time begun to feel a distinction from the rest of the Oxford Groupers, acquired an identity and a name for themselves. The A.A. groups grew simultaneously in New York and Akron as more and more drunks were brought into the Oxford Group through the efforts of Bill, Dr. Bob, and the newly-sober proselytes. As it became uncomfortably apparent that there were distinct differences between the needs of the alcoholics and those of the other Oxford Groupers, tensions grew. Finally, the New York A.A.'s split away in 1937, and the Akron A.A.'s moved away in 1939.

After the split, groups calling themselves Alcoholics Anonymous began to spring up in increasing numbers as alcoholics carried the program back home from visits to Akron or New York. It is often said of that time that all that was needed to start an A.A. group was a coffee pot and a resentment.

The fellowship got much needed national attention in 1941, when the *Saturday Evening Post* featured it in a story by Jack Alexander in its March 1 issue. That was the breakthrough they needed. They now had national recognition.

By 1950, the fellowship was large enough to have its first International Convention, held in Cleveland. At this convention, the Twelve Traditions were formally adopted. A.A. was firmly established as an anonymous fellowship that did not exist for profit. The first International was Dr. Bob's last appearance. He was dying of cancer and could barely stand up at the podium. His last talk demonstrates the clarity and precision of a man who has distilled the wisdom of his lifetime:

"There are two or three things that flashed into my mind on which it would be fitting to lay a little emphasis. One is the simplicity of our program. Let's not louse it all up with Freudian complexes and things that are interesting to the scientific mind, but have very little to do with our actual A.A. work. Our Twelve Steps, when simmered down to the last, resolve themselves into the words 'love' and 'service.' We understand what love is, and we understand what service is. So let's bear those two things in mind.

"Let us also remember to guard that erring member the tongue, and if we must use it, let's use it with kindness and consideration and tolerance.

"And one more thing: None of us would be here today if somebody hadn't taken time to explain things to us, to give us a little pat on the back, to take us to a meeting or two, to do numerous little kind and thoughtful acts in our behalf. So let us never get such a degree of smug complacency that we're not willing to extend, or attempt to extend, to our less fortunate brothers that help which has been so beneficial to us."

Dr. Bob died November 16, 1950. His beloved Anne had died June 1, 1949 and he had suffered acutely in his last year.

In 1955 the second International was held in St. Louis. At this conference, Bill turned A.A. over to the A.A.'s. A.A. was now independent of him, standing solidly by itself on the Twelve Steps and Twelve Traditions, on principles, not personalities.

Bill Wilson was to live another 16 years, and write prolifically. When he died, on January 24, 1971, he left several books describing in detail his role in A.A.. His wife Lois remained active as an A.A. spokesperson and Al-Anon matriarch until her death in 1988. She is credited with having formally started the family groups—Al-Anon and Alateen—in 1951 and 1957 after both Dr. Bob and Anne had died. Bill and Lois had no children. They left a house in New York, "Stepping Stones." Dr. Bob and Anne were survived by their children, Sue and Bob ("Smitty").

SUE'S STORY

PREFACE TO SUE'S STORY

Suzanne Smith Windows was born February 15, 1918. Later in her life she was informed that her biological mother, unable to support her or her infant sister, had turned the children over to their maternal grandmother at a young age. The maternal grandmother quickly gave up both children to the Summit County (OH) Children's Home. Sue's earliest memory appears to be the walk to the home with her grandmother and infant sister at age 3. Sue's original name was "Winona Mary."

Sue was adopted by Doctor Bob and Anne Smith in the summer of 1923 at age 5. She spent the next 17 years living with them and her step-brother Smitty in the Smith house on Ardmore Avenue.

She became close friends with Ray Windows, the son of an alcoholic janitor, at age 12. Her parents began to oppose the relationship as she grew older and she was forbidden to see him. Her teen years were marked by her attachment to Ray and the development of various subterfuges to see him in spite of her parents' opposition.

In the autumn of 1935 she met Ernie W. Galbraith, a divorced man 14 years her senior with an adolescent son, Ernie, Jr., from an earlier marriage. Ernie was A.A. #4, one of the early "pigeons" for the fledgling program just born in Akron that summer. Sue remembers that Dr. Bob encouraged Ernie to take an interest in her.

Sue graduated from high school in June, 1936. In the same year, Ray Windows left to work with the Civilian Conservation Corps in California. Gradually, Ernie Galbraith asserted his claim to Sue and in late 1937 he told Ray Windows to leave Sue alone. At the same time, Dr. Bob began his opposition to Sue's attachment to Ernie. The escalation of this conflict grew until January 1941 when Sue left the house on Ardmore to live in a rented room.

In September, 1941, at age 23, Sue married Ernie Galbraith, who was 37, at a ceremony attended only by his parents. Her own parents had not been on speaking terms with her since her decision to move away from Ardmore Avenue. Sue herself repaired what she could of the relationship by calling on her mother on December 7, 1941, offering assistance to Anne who had broken her ankle.

Sue's first child, Mickey, was born in April 1944. Her daughter, Bonna Lee, was born 18 months later in October of 1945, shortly after Sue and Ernie moved into the house in Akron where Sue still resides today.

Sue was stricken with acute agoraphobia in the period 1947-1948 when her children reached the age she herself was at the time of her abandonment to the orphanage. On one occasion, Bill Wilson tried to help her out of it, and she tried various cures including medication and professional counseling. Throughout the rest of her life she has battled the condition with varying degrees of success.

Sue and Ernie accompanied Bill and Lois Wilson to the Second A.A. International in St. Louis in 1955. Although Ernie was included as one of the original A.A. starters, his recovery was always shaky and he relapsed into active, progressive drinking. His story was removed from the Big Book with the Second Edition.

Ernie's alcohol addiction and infidelity finally pushed Sue to separate and then divorce him in 1965. Their daughter Bonna was married in 1962, and gave birth to a daughter, Sandy, in October of that year, one day before her 17th birthday. Bonna divorced her husband in 1965. The notice of Bonna's divorce was published in the local newspaper on the same day as Sue and Ernie's.

Mickey was married in 1964, had a daughter in 1967, another daughter in 1968, and a son in 1970. His first marriage was dissolved in later years, and he is now remarried and living in Tennessee.

12

Bonna led an unsettled life and remarried in March 1969. She and her daughter Sandy, age 6, died tragically on June 11, 1969, near Akron. Ernie Galbraith died two years later to the day, June 11, 1971.

Sue worked at the library at Kent State University for many years after her divorce from Ernie. She began to participate in the Founder's Day activities and maintained her friendship with Bill and Lois.

Ray Windows renewed his attachment to her in October, 1975, after the death of his wife. After seeing each other for two months, he and Sue were married on December 19, 1975, in Akron.

Sue retired from Kent State and became active in the Founder's Foundation restoration of the house on Ardmore Avenue. Sue and Ray devoted much of their time to the project. They also attended the A.A. International in Montreal in 1985.

Ray, after suffering from lung cancer and circulatory disease for several years, died on August 3, 1989. Sue remains in her house in Akron, still in close contact with the remnants of the founding of the A.A. fellowship in Akron.

1
THE ADOPTION

The first thing I remember is walking down a railroad track with an older woman who was carrying a baby. The woman was my grandmother, I found out later. She couldn't afford to keep us anymore.

I don't remember too much about the Children's Home except being rapped on the knuckles with a ruler because I didn't put my slipper away. I can't remember what the place looked like or who took care of me. After I got there, I must have shut my mind to things. I don't remember. Once I got one of my fingers caught in the toilet door, and I chopped the end of it off. I think Dr. Bob might have been the doctor who came. That would have been when he first saw me, and it was the nicest day of my life. I was five.

The day Dr. Bob came to get me, we drove up to Akron City Hospital, which, at the time, had a big circular drive. He had to make a call, and he told me, "Sit in that car, and don't move." So I sat there, staring at the dials on the dashboard, afraid to breathe.

I must have been scared because that was my nature. I didn't know I was being adopted. I didn't know anything. I just knew I was being removed from one place and put into another. I still get scared when I'm not sure what's going to happen.

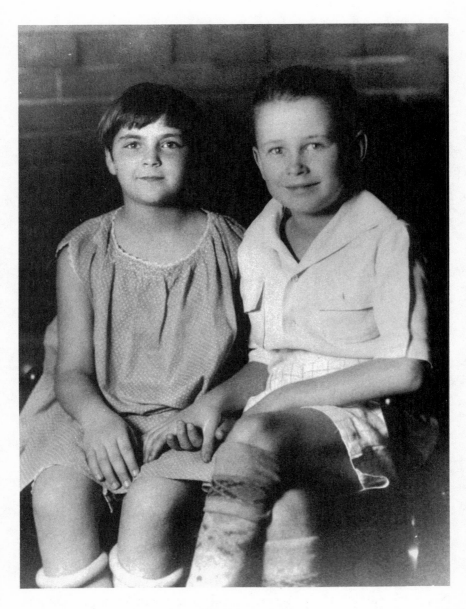

Sue and Smitty at age 5.

We went home then, to the house on Ardmore Avenue. It looked big to me, but it was like a real home: flowered wallpaper, fringed lamps, worn-out old oriental rugs, and a big, white kitchen. I remember it was warm and we had potato soup for supper that night. I put on a new pinafore.

At first I was very insecure. I remember when I first got there mom would be working in her flower garden and she'd go around the side of the house where I couldn't see her. I'd sit on the back steps and bawl because I thought she was gone. I couldn't let her out of my sight. I followed her everywhere.

My mother was a heavyset woman, and wore her dark hair pulled back in a bun. She had the bluest eyes. She loved big, fancy hats and classical music. She was kind of artistic, and did watercolors, crafts, and beautiful smocking. She was very intelligent, too. She always listened to the political conventions on the radio, which we hated. She wasn't a pretty woman, and she dressed very plain. She had a nice disposition.

When I was real little, I'd sit on my mom's lap, I remember, and look at her ring. The light from the old fringed floor lamp would shine on it, and we'd sit and look at the different colors. It fascinated me. We would just sit and talk. At that time, Smitty was more outgoing. He was beginning to edge away from home a little, so I got more of her attention, I guess.

My mother's family was very well off. Her three brothers were all in the Who's Who, but two of them never spoke to her because of something that happened at my grandmother's funeral, I believe. I don't know what it was and never did find out. I don't want to know. I just know they never spoke to each other. And she would never talk about it.

She always spoke of how she loved her mother, who died before Smitty was born. Dad used to tell us how Grandmother Ripley would come to stay a week or two every year and do all the cleaning and cooking and sew clothes. And then she'd say, "Well, time to go," and leave. I never got to see her, of course; she was gone way before I got there.

I wrote to one of my uncles once, the friendly one, to ask about Mom's family tree. Then Dad tried to visit one of them when he was in New York with Bill, to try to make amends. The first thing the guy said was, "Well, what do *you* want?" Dad said the guy treated him as if he had come to borrow money. So Mom didn't have much family except for Dad and us. We were it.

Anne Smith as a young woman in a pose
typical of the times, around 1910.

Mother was always home. When we were little she never went away, and if she did, we either went next door for lunch or to the stores at Highland Square in Akron. Every morning I'd get dressed for school and go down to the kitchen. I wasn't much of a breakfast eater. I just don't like breakfast, period. But I'd sit with them 'til it was time to go to school. Smitty would be there, and he ate breakfast. Mom would listen to the Breakfast Club on the radio, and drink her coffee. Dad would be still in bed. He usually didn't go out until about 10 a.m. Mom would talk to us. I couldn't tell you anything she said, but she probably saw to it that we had our books or whatever we had to take to school. She made me wear these cotton-picking woolen hose. I couldn't stand them. I'd get a few blocks away from home and I'd roll them down.

Mom was home when we got home and we always had something to eat, usually milk and cookies. Then we went out to play. When we were really little, you could usually find us in the sandbox next door. But we did have quite a bit of freedom for kids. We were out all the time.

Mother wasn't very well. She had an early hysterectomy, and could not have another child. I think she had that when I was about nine years old. We went to the hospital to see her one time, and this friend of ours from school was there because his dad was in the hospital, too. We all went out in the hall and started racing in the wheelchairs.

Mom wasn't an active person, sportwise. She was very intelligent; she read a lot. She liked Agatha Christie mysteries. She was more the kind who would read to you. *Winnie the Pooh* was a favorite. Or she would see to it that you had something to do. She was creative. One time for Sunday school we made decorated crosses with shells on them that were real pretty.

I liked to help Mom in the garden in the backyard. When I got older, she'd have me dig it up every year, and every year I would say, "Well, what about this thing or that?" She'd be standing there in her old sun hat and say, "Well, if it's worth anything, it will come back up."

I feel kind of guilty in a way about my feelings about my mom because it seemed to me I always got along better with my dad than my mother. But the more I think about things, the more I see that she was there when I really needed her. When I was real little, when I was hurt or sick or anything, I probably went to Mom because Dad was at work. He'd be out and Mom was always there. I tried to do things that would make it easier for her. When she had her hysterectomy, I started to cook and do some housework.

If we'd get sick or anything, my dad would go to the drugstore and get us comic books. When he came home from work most times he had a pack of Lifesavers for us. He'd make us reach in his coat pocket, and get them. We really looked forward to him coming home. Now, Smitty tells me that Dad had the Lifesavers to hide the liquor on his breath, but I don't remember that.

Sue and Smitty in the neighbor's sandbox.

2
MY DAD, DR. BOB

I idolized my dad. He was it. I think you could say I was a "Daddy's girl." We used to play cards together or sit and talk or we'd wrestle. We'd do a lot of different things. And he had those tattoos on his arms. He had a big compass on his arm, along with a dragon. When I was little I used to sit on his lap, and he would read off every one of those 32 points on the compass. It used to fascinate me.

We'd go to movies together. You could have fun with my dad. He used to play tennis with Smitty and me and he'd wear us out. He loved to drive down country roads. Sometimes if Mom didn't want to go for a ride on Sunday afternoon, we'd go down one of those old country roads where the weeds came up over the running board. We never knew where we were going until we'd run into a creek or something.

One time the dog got in a fight with a skunk, and my dad brought him home on the running board. You could smell skunk in the house for months after that. Dad cried when that dog died. You could see the tears in his eyes. The dog got hit by a car; in fact, he's buried by the house on Ardmore Avenue.

I used to go to the hospital with Dad on Sunday mornings. The only other thing I had to do on Sundays was peel the potatoes for dinner. I'd peel, and then I'd be ready to go to the hospital with my dad. On the way over he always used to stop at this grocery store and there would be a guy, a foreign fellow, who had wine, and he would get wine on Sundays. I didn't realize that until a lot later.

I used to go over to the hospital while Dad was making his calls, and I'd talk to the nurses in the emergency room. I really enjoyed being with my dad. I always thought I'd be a good nurse. But my dad didn't think so, I guess. He had it fixed with "Old Cranz" over at the hospital that they would tell me I was too short, which is a crock.

I thought my dad was a real brain. He insisted we speak good English. I didn't always do it, but he helped us a lot. I'd watch him work those cross-word puzzles, and he taught me to work them, too. He said, "If you can't entertain yourself, you're poor company with anybody." I always kept that in mind, and I can entertain myself to this day.

I was a little bit scared of my dad. In fact, I was plenty scared of him because 6'4" looked pretty big when I was little. Even now, 6'4" looks pretty big from down here at 5 feet! And he had a heavy voice, a strong voice. He could cut you up with it when you needed it. But he was never rough. He was a gentle man. I'm not saying he didn't paddle us when we needed it. He did. We didn't get it often, but when we did, we knew we had earned it.

When I was told to do something, I did it. They didn't really order me around too much when I was real little, except when I got nasty. When either Smitty or I did get nasty, we got a good paddling. I was scared of that paddle, and my dad was scared of our dog. We had to shut the door at the top of the steps when we got a paddling because the dog would grab him if he thought Dad was hurting us kids.

The paddle Dad used on us came from a game that had a ball with it. One end of the paddle was big and one end was little. Dad used the little end, the part that hurt like the dickens. Mom would use the big end; it didn't hurt as much for some reason. Well, Dad found out and he whittled it down so that both ends were the same. He always kept that paddle on an inside shelf of the bathroom closet. It was about a half-inch thick. Like I say, when we got it, we knew it.

Smitty and Sue with Roger,
a pit bull who had to be muzzled to prevent
attacks on the neighbors' dogs.

When Dr. Bob got "Old Cranz" to tell Sue she was too short to be a nurse, he may have been telling the truth. In this photograph of Dr. Bob as an intern with the nurses, notice their height. He was 6'4".

24

I remember one time I licked some postage stamps and put them on the pages of a book as I was sitting on the floor. Of course I lied about it to my mom, and when Dad got back, I got a whipping. I had my choice. I could either have a whipping or I could stay in my room. I took the whipping.

As we got older, my dad would try and do family things. We had a cottage out on the lake. My mother couldn't swim a stroke, but she taught us all how to swim.

Dad had feelings, too. A little girl drowned out at the cottage one year. He was real upset about it. We had a maid, and her little sister was at the cottage with us. I don't remember why we had her but we did. She often followed me. We had a boat house right in front of the place, and a little path went up some steps up the bank to the house. Right next to it, there was a dock that was partly under water. It was cement and it had that green slime on it. She and I were going up to the house for something. I started up the steps but when I got to the house, she wasn't there. I just assumed that the kid was in back of me, that she was going to run up the steps the same way I did. I didn't know when she left or anything. Finally, Mother asked me, "Where is so-and-so?" And I said, "I don't know; she was right with me." So we began to piece things together, and we figured that dock under water attracted her in some way and she went in. They had to dive for her.

I probably wasn't more than seven or eight. I can't remember whether we ever went back after that or not. But I know my dad felt terrible about it.

I never figured out how she died. I just overheard them talking. No one ever talked to me about it. Of course I remember the people out there trying to dive for her. You remember things like that.

It was real upsetting. But I didn't blame myself, because I didn't know what had happened to her. I hadn't asked her to follow me or anything. She said she was coming, so I said, "Come on," and we went. I thought she was behind me. I didn't feel guilty about it, but it scared me. I felt bad about it, but I didn't feel guilty.

3

SYMPTOMS OF THE SECOND STAGE

I was about 13 or 14 when I first started to have trouble with Dad's drinking. Maybe if the family had been more stable, things wouldn't have been so edgy. It seemed like everybody was on edge. Mom was on edge because of Dad. Dad was on edge because of his drinking. Smitty felt bad because he felt like he was poor and I was on edge because I felt they were against my friends and they wouldn't let me see my boyfriend Ray Windows.

Over the weekends I would have my buddy Barb stay over at my house, or I'd stay over at her house. When we stayed at my house, we'd play cards, fix our hair, and listen to the dance bands. They had them on the radio then, and we enjoyed listening to them and playing cards.

I loved the bands—Clyde McCoy, the Dorseys, Ben Bernie, Guy Lombardo, Henry Busse. They'd play all my favorite songs like "Dark Eyes," "Whispering," and "I Don't Know Why." And we'd sit there at the dining room table until 2:00 in the morning. We could sleep late, and we had Saturday off, and I'd done whatever cleaning I had to do.

A couple of times Dad would get real nasty about making us go to bed. And he'd jump all over my friends. He'd get pretty mean when it seemed like all we were doing was having fun. One time he said to Barb, "One more peep out of you, young lady, and you'll go home." Well, that irritated me no end, you know, and embarrassed me. I asked my mom, "Why does he do that?" After I asked her that a few times, she finally told me that he was drinking, and he couldn't go down to the basement to his supply when we were up. Like I told him later, "You could have had umpteen bottles down there, and we wouldn't have known the difference." But I think, his behavior was more the alcohol talking.

We never said anything about Dad's drinking. When you get told that you had better do what they tell you as long as you're under their roof, you don't argue. You don't even try. I know one time I squawked—this was even after I had a job—because I couldn't see why I always had to be the one that had to do the darn dishes all the time. And he got those steely blue eyes and that hard voice and he said, "Young lady, if you don't like the way it is, you can move." So you just didn't bring up any of your dislikes. At least I didn't.

I remember one time, I think it was during the day, when he was having a hangover and he wanted a drink. He had a '27 Cadillac at the time, and he parked it at the minister's house several doors down. Dad was upstairs in bed and the room was dark. I went up and he called me in and asked me to go down the street and get him a bottle out of the car. I knew he was in bad shape, needing a drink. He had that look. But I told him, no, I wasn't going to do it. Well, he started offering me money. He said $10. And this was the Depression when $10 was a fortune! I still wouldn't do it.

Then he started getting a little nasty and sarcastic, with that voice of his. I still wouldn't go. I said Mama wouldn't like it. He said something like Mama wasn't the one that needed it. And of course, you couldn't get sarcastic back, because then he got nastier and you couldn't win. He was beginning to get that way. He could just cut you up with that sarcastic voice. Afterward, I guess he had it on his conscience. He would sneak in and add dimes to my bank. I'd find them there.

You could see mother was getting despondent and was losing her friends. They weren't coming over. They didn't want to get in that mess. But to me it wasn't really a mess because he was upstairs, and he wasn't bothering anybody. He wasn't a drunk that stuck his tongue out at the neighbors and called them names and used foul language or things like that. He didn't do that kind of stuff. He just was not bringing the money home. And there was the worry of not knowing where he was, when he was going to come home, if he was going to come home, and that type of thing.

27

He wasn't usually one of those drunks that went out drinking somewhere. But I remember one time when it was raining and I was coming home from school on the bus. I went by the bar and his car was there. It went fleetingly through my mind but didn't really register. I went home and sat down to dinner, and pretty soon Mom started saying, "Well, I wonder where Dad is?" It was the strangest thing, but it never occurred to me to tell her I'd seen the car. I just didn't make the connection. After dinner I started washing the dishes, and it got dark. It was still raining. And she just kept it up, asking where he might be. And finally I thought of it. I said, "You know, I do remember seeing his car down at that bar." So Smitty put on his raincoat and walked down there with an old umbrella and that's where he was. That's the only time I remember him being out at a bar. Smitty says Dad would check himself into a hotel and stay out when he was drinking, but I don't remember that.

I do remember helping him up the stairs. It took the three of us to do it —Smitty pulling, and me and Mom pushing. Mom wasn't really well; she'd had the hysterectomy. Smitty was stronger, and I was strong myself, but I wasn't strong enough to take on a 6'4" guy.

Like I say, Mom was down. She'd sit over in the corner of the kitchen in her apron and smoke cigarettes. She always criticized his mother for Dad's drinking. And she told Smitty and me that if it wasn't for us kids, she probably would commit suicide.

But after the Oxford Group she simmered down. She always had hope. She said she didn't care if it was the Holy Rollers that straightened him up, as long as something did.

Henrietta Seiberling got Mom into the Oxford Group sometime in 1932. I don't know how they met, but Henrietta was a good friend. Mom had other friends from the Oxford Group helping her too. Clarace Williams was a good friend, and the group met at her house. Then there was a little old gal who was a schoolteacher. She actually married one of my classmates.

After the Oxford Group, Mom didn't sit in the corner of the kitchen smoking so much. She moved the ashtray to the telephone in the dining room. She spent a lot of time talking to her friends. She had that outlet. Later on, she did the same thing with the A.A. women. She did pass on the help that she received to the other women. And I think that was the start of Al-Anon.

28

I've still got Mom's notebook from the Oxford Group meetings. I typed up a lot of it myself for my typing practice. If you read it, you'd see why Bill W. called her "the Mother of A.A.," and what I mean about my mom being the founder of Al-Anon. It's all there—share with people, don't preach, don't argue, don't talk up or down to people, share in terms of your own experience, be willing to live a day at a time, an hour at a time, surrender, pray for guidance, and have a daily meditation time. She was a very intelligent person, and she knew what she was putting down in her notes. Lois and Bill took this notebook with them one time after they read it. It was when they stayed at the house when Dad died. I did get it back eventually, but parts were missing.

If it hadn't been for the Oxford Group, I don't know what would have happened. The Oxford Group gave Mother the incentive to keep going. She couldn't really give up, though, since she had nowhere else to go.

Sometime in 1933, Henrietta and another lady got the idea for Mom to bring Dad over to the meeting, so she did. He liked the boys and what-have-you, he shared his alcoholism with the group, and he did change some, but he still drank. It just wasn't quite as open. Things were better. I could see the change in Mom. Not only that, but I knew that if I didn't want to go to the meeting I could stay home and see Ray. That was when the window shade came in handy. I'd use the shade in my room to signal Ray.

Even then, it was hard for me to fool my dad. He always knew what was going on, like with the smoking. I started smoking when I was 12. My mother said she could tell there was something going on because I would get sleepy. She tried to talk me out of it, and, of course, I sneaked and kept doing it. My girlfriend Barb would come up to my room. I had movie star pictures all over the place. You couldn't even see the wallpaper anymore. We'd go up there and read movie magazines and smoke. One time Dad came in, and although we hadn't had a cigarette right away, you know how smoke lingers, especially in a small room like that. He came around and looked at the pictures, and said, "My, nice pictures," and he kept sniffing. We knew what he was doing, but he didn't scold us.

So when I was 16, I think it was, Dad and I went out one time for a hamburger. Sometimes we'd go out for a hamburger, even without too much money, because they were cheap. Swenson's sold them for about 20 or 25 cents. Anyhow, we ate in the car, and after we were through, he lit a cigarette and handed it to me. He didn't say a word. I about fainted. From then on, I could smoke openly.

We had to steal Mother's butts, you know. Mom would leave big ones. Then she got a roll-your-own machine. We would roll them for her, and we'd put pencil shavings in them. They would burn up when she lit one, and she would say, "I don't think these are as good as the packaged kind." Then she'd go back to the packaged kind, which we liked better. It took her a while to catch on. My brother and I were not a joy.

I guess I was pretty rebellious. And I was resentful. It goes back to them not liking the people I went around with. They decided they didn't like Ray the minute we started going together. When we were in grade school we didn't play together, we just went to school together. They didn't bother about him then. But then we started going together. I think it was right after we'd graduated from grade school. That was when the trouble started.

It started with the ball games we'd have outside in the street. We had people from 5 or 6 years old up to my dad's age, you know—all ages and sizes. But Dad didn't come out very often.

I used to get Mom to let me put the dishes away in the oven to get them out of the way, so in case company came over, the dishes wouldn't be around. That way I'd get to go out and play ball right after dinner. I had to do them when I came in, which was all right with me. I was ready to do them then. We just played ball in the street, and we had a good time.

Then one night, Ray and his brother and a couple of other guys walked around while we were playing ball. They hung back, just watching, and then after a while, they joined us. That's how Ray started coming around. This happened almost every night in the summertime, playing ball until the fireflies came out. And we just gradually got to going together. We were both lonesome, I guess.

That was around 1932. I guess I was 13, 14 maybe. My parents thought Ray was hanging around too much. He was small and quiet and shy, like me. He looked at his toes when he talked. When he would come by himself, for a while they'd let him come in, but then they didn't. I think maybe my dad might have relented in time, but Mom was always harping at him. She just didn't like him.

They wouldn't tell me exactly why, because they didn't want me to know they were snobs. Mom was, socially speaking. She was a doctor's wife and she thought that we had a position to uphold or something. Back then, that's about all we had. I remember there was another fellow that came around at the same time and he was sweet on me. He was from a prominent Akron family. But I didn't like him. He parted his hair in the middle and had a goofy smile. He was half nuts. He's still half nuts. But I think my mother would have accepted him more than Ray because of Ray's background.

Ray's dad was a janitor and the family wasn't well educated. They were from Pennsylvania. His dad had worked in the coal mines. Then they came to Akron, and I don't think his dad was very active. My parents thought he was lazy, and they thought Ray would be, too. Also, there was the belief that if you marry someone who is in the trades or a real hard-working man, that when they get home all they want is sex and a lot of kids. And I don't think they wanted that for me either.

I was forbidden to see Ray, but I did it anyhow. I can see they thought we were too much of the same nature. Ray was shy, and so was I. He wasn't exactly what you'd call a wheel in school. Of course, I wasn't a whiz either. I had to study like hell to get my lessons, but once I got it, I remembered it. But it took me a long time. That was another thing. I overheard my mom say one time I wasn't college material. So you figure right off you're a dummy.

I think they were projecting and I was objecting. One time when I was about 16 or 17, Dad went over to Ray's. Ray said, "When I crossed the street, I tried to ignore him, but he wasn't going to be ignored that day." Dad cornered Ray and told him they didn't want me to see him because they were losing control over me at home. I suppose they thought they were losing control because I defied them so much about seeing Ray. They weren't there much, either one of them, and I still did the housework and stuff like that. I never minded doing the housework, although I hate it now.

I did almost all the household chores. I had to change the beds and run the sweeper and pick up clothes. Then on Monday night, I had to soak the clothes. We did have a laundress—a colored woman named Lizzie. We had her for years. She would come once a week, and she did that whole laundry in one day, ironing and everything. I did the dishes every night, peeled the

31

potatoes for dinner, got the vegetables ready, and once a week I'd plan an entire meal and cook it.

Mom was a good cook. I don't think she really liked to cook, but she was good. She showed me how to make angel food cake and I would make them for the neighbors for 35 cents. They would supply all the makin's.

Smitty mowed the lawn every couple of weeks. I didn't think the work was evenly distributed, but then he had outside interests. If I'd had outside interests I probably wouldn't have had to do all the chores, but I was too bashful. And they didn't like the people I ran around with, so I just hung around the house.

I started doing the chores for my allowance in seventh grade. I used to take that allowance and walk down to a movie theater every Saturday afternoon. A lot of the kids from school would come down. We'd meet and have an ice cream cone or a candy bar or something. It was a Saturday matinee strictly for kids.

We did a lot of walking in those days. I never did have a bicycle. If I rode a bicycle, I borrowed it. And I don't think they would ever have taught me how to drive because I think they were afraid I'd go pick up Ray. So I never learned to drive 'til after I was married the first time.

Ray and I had to start sneaking around almost as soon as we started going together. Barb used to help us. She was a friend up until the day she died. Mom and Dad liked her, but they knew that she was helping me. They knew what was going on. I would go over to the library—the old library trick—with a lot of books that I never read, and Ray would be there.

Ray lived on a corner in the apartments where his Dad was the janitor. They always used to sit around on the corner, watch people go by, and just pass the time. That's another thing my dad didn't like. There was a drugstore right across the street, and an ice cream store. And of course, if I had to have an ice cream cone or something from the drugstore, I had to go right by there and I'd see Ray. If I borrowed a bicycle, I'd ride over that way. Later on, when I couldn't get out, I'd pull my window shade a certain way, and he'd know that I couldn't make it that night. If the shade was up, he'd know I'd probably be able to get out.

Ray would come over to Barb's when I was staying at her house for the weekend. One time, when I was supposed to be at Barb's, I went out for a Sunday drive with Ray and a friend of his who had a car. When I got back,

Barb said, "Well, the thing that I always thought would happen has happened. Your mom and dad called, and you weren't here." They'd called a couple of times. I knew I was shot.

So they came over and got me, and I really got it then. I didn't get whipped, but I got a good tongue-lashing. I was about 15. I don't think Dad was in A.A. yet. He told me that "as long as you live in my house, young lady, you're going to do as I say." It was the old Vermont chill—he could do it with that voice and those steely blue eyes.

When they said all that, I defied them. I just thought, well, who the heck do you like? They don't like anybody I go around with. I've got to go around with somebody. I'm not just going to stick around the house by myself.

They didn't like what I was doing, even though it wasn't anything bad —just going to movies, playing ball, and taking walks and rides. We weren't going to motels or anything like that.

I remember one time when I was a little bit older, I went out with Barb and her boyfriend. I had a couple of drinks, and I wasn't a drinker. I was really getting dizzy. I was mad at my family, and my friends didn't drive me home.

I went to the neighbor's and I stayed there for two or three days. I didn't know what else I could do. Finally my mother called and told me to get my fanny home. I must have been 17. I was probably fighting with them about Ray. Dad was drinking, Mom was upset about Dad, Smitty was upset because we were poor, and I was upset about Ray.

Sue at age 15 or 16,
deeply interested in Ray Windows.

4

BILL MEETS DR. BOB

I was 17 in 1935, the year Bill W. came to Akron. Dad had been going to Oxford Group meetings, but they just didn't work since he was the only drunk there. Bill W. had come to town for a proxy fight, and he lost it. He says that the people he came with went back to New York and left him stranded with only $10. That was when he had to decide whether to make the call or go get drunk. He decided that he would look for some Oxford Groupers in Akron.

He looked down the church directory and picked Dr. Tunks because of the name. It was a funny name, so Bill thought he'd call him just on that basis. He called and asked if there were any Oxford Groups in the church, and Dr. Tunks said, "Yes, I do have a chapter there," and gave him a list of names.

Now in a lot of books they show a picture of the phone booth, and I do believe he made that first call from that phone booth. But when Dr. Tunks gave him the names of these people, Bill went up to his room, because I don't think he had that many nickels to spare. Calls from his room could go on the bill, you know. He called several people and everybody was either out of town or busy since it was Mother's Day.

He finally got down to Norman Sheppard and Norman said he was getting ready to go out of town. But, he said, if you call Henrietta Seiberling, she will talk to you. So that's what Bill did. He thought, well, Seiberling is a big name. Surely it couldn't be the old boy's wife, because she would be too old. She wouldn't be doing anything like that. So he called Henrietta, and she invited him out for lunch, and after that she called Mother. Dad had come home in the meantime.

I wasn't home. I was probably downtown at the show with Ray or something. But anyhow, there is something I have to clear up. Bill always says that Dad was potted under the table, but that is not so. My dad wasn't that kind of drunk. He was potted, that's for sure, but I never saw dad fall in his life. And if he did get drunk, he never drove home. He always had the boys at Central Garage drive him home so he wouldn't have an accident. Anyhow, he had gone up to bed. He was not under the table.

Another point is that Norman Sheppard said for years that he was the one who gave Henrietta's name to Bill. Other people thought that Henrietta's name was on the list that Dr. Tunks gave him. Well, I believe that Norman Sheppard did give Henrietta Seiberling's name to Bill. Maybe it's not a real important fact, but if you let some things slip, other things are going to slip, and eventually there's going to be no true story.

Anyway, they called Mother. They wanted Dad to come over to Henrietta's house, and Mother said no. She said, "Bob is in no shape." So Henri (my dad called her Henri), being a very persistent gal, made Mom promise to bring him over the next day—or Mom offered to. Henri says that Mom promised to have him over there the next day, and Dad says that she only agreed to try. So I am inclined to believe Dad.

Smitty went over with them the next day. I didn't. I was at our house because I wanted to see Ray even though they said they would only be gone for 15 minutes. I figured it would be longer than that. If I had known it was going to be four or five hours, I'd have had a ball.

When Dad got up that day, he was real shaky. I was standing at the living room window watching them when they drove away. Of course I was always there when they left. It was five-something in the afternoon when they left, and it was after 1 a.m. when they came home. They said 11 p.m., but it was after 1 a.m. because I was really getting worried about them.

Ray had to be home by 10:00. I was waiting alone. When they came in, I just told them I had been getting worried about them. They said they had no idea they were going to be this late, and they trotted off to bed.

The next day, we were out pulling weeds in the garden and Mom mentioned that she finally had some hope, that this might be a turning point. Dad had talked to her about his discussion with Bill and she just pounced on it. She thought they were onto something.

I started noticing some changes about two weeks after because Bill came over to live with us. That was a big change. Bill stayed at the Portage Country Club for two weeks, and then Mom told me and Smitty that Bill was coming to stay with us, that she'd invited him, and that it would help both Dad and Bill a lot.

I didn't get thrown out of my room. Smitty and Mom usually slept in the twin bedroom. This was because Dad could not sleep at night and he would be getting up to go down and get his bottle all the time. So then, when Bill came, he got Dad's room, Dad went into the twin bedroom with Mom, and Smitty got relegated to the attic. That was the time Smitty got the doggoned screech owl. I don't know where Smitty got it; he found it somewhere. It screeched all night. After about the third night dad said, "That thing's got to go." So it went. Dad took it out to the woods. He didn't hurt it or anything.

Bill would come down in the morning and make the coffee; it was good coffee. He was an early riser, and he smoked a lot. He'd put that cigarette in the corner of his mouth and he'd squint at you through the smoke. I also remember him putting up his feet and we'd see a big hole in his shoe. And he had Mom put two full whiskey bottles on the kitchen counter. That drove her crazy, but he wanted to prove a point that he could have it there and not drink.

In a way, Bill sort of ignored us kids. He didn't have any kids of his own, and he talked more with Mom and Dad. Smitty and I had our own interests and we were going in and out all the time, and Bill would say "hello," you know, something friendly. But nobody ever sat down and told us what was going on.

Dr. Bob on the back steps, around 1935.
Anne's garden can be seen at left.

Back then, kids were not talked to. We were supposed to be quiet and stay out of the way. So I was quiet and I wasn't in the way, but I heard what was said. I'd hear Bill and Dad or Bill and Mom talking. I'd go into the kitchen or the living room or I'd be sitting at the dining room table doing a crossword puzzle, and they'd be there talking. They'd stay up until 2:00 in the morning, just talking.

I was just a bystander, until it came time to make the coffee. Then I was A#1 dog, putting the coffee water on. I could walk into the room anytime when they were talking and there wouldn't even be a break in the conversation. So I'd go in and have a cup of coffee, too. That's how I started drinking coffee. In fact, even the dog drank coffee out of a saucer. I still have that coffee pot— the one we used when Bill and Dad first got together.

I was usually there, except when Bill would play that damned violin. Then Smitty and I would take off. Smitty didn't have a violin, but I took a couple of lessons once and that was enough for me. In fact, I finally ended up giving it to the Children's Home. But Bill said he played so we let him use it. And there was so much squeaking and squawking that we got out of there. He was bad, I'll tell you.

At the time Bill first came, I was still in school. I remember school got out around June fifth because I went to Ray's graduation while Dad was getting sobered up from his last drunk. Ray graduated from Hower Trade School on June 7, 1935. I finally convinced my dad to let me go to Ray's graduation. Dad didn't want me to. But he did give up and let me go because that was the weekend after the Atlantic City convention when he had his last slip. He was stuck in bed getting sobered up for the operation he had to perform. I think it was more for his own nerves that he let me go, just to keep me from pestering him to death.

Mom dreaded Dad going to Atlantic City. She just dreaded it. She had that feeling, and it turned out she was right. When he did come home smashed, she was really crushed. She sat at the kitchen table, lighting one cigarette off another, while Bill kept trying to reassure her. She just thought that Dad had lost it all even though Bill had slipped, too, after Ebby first talked to him. When Dad came back, he was in bed for two or three days. Mom was very upset. Then she let Bill take over. Bill kept assuring her that it would work, that it was a different approach. Dad was really sheepish. He could look real hangdog, you know. Like I said, I kept going up there and pestering him about Ray's graduation. First he said he'd think about it, and of course, I kept at him and at him, and he finally let me go.

Mom didn't think too much of it, but she went along with him. She always did. Like my friend Elgie said, "Whatever Doc said was fine with Anne." She used to say my mother was just a shadow of my father. But there was a lot more there.

The graduation was on a Friday, and it was a nice evening. Ray's mother and dad and a friend of his came by and picked me up. I stood at the door, watching for them though the lace curtains, so I could just run out when they pulled up. We were all dressed up, and we went down to some big hall. This was the Depression and we didn't have that much. I borrowed a pair of my mother's good T-strap shoes. But no hat; I never wore hats. I still don't.

I sat with Ray's family and watched him get his diploma. Then they had to take me home. Since I was allowed to do that much, I'd knew I'd better kowtow a little. When I got home they asked me how it was and I told them I enjoyed it. But they weren't exactly enthused. I went up to my room and kept it to myself.

After Dad got back from the Atlantic City convention, Bill had worked on him, getting him ready for the operation he was supposed to do. I wasn't in the bedroom when Dad took his beer before the operation, but Bill told me he took it. Bill came down to get the beer. We knew it was in the refrigerator, and when Bill took it out, Mom didn't exactly go for that. But Bill told her, "This'll be the last one. He's going to go to the hospital and do his operation and he'll be back." I think he gave it to Dad before he got up, because Dad was always kind of shaky. That was his last drink.

It was Monday, June 10. I saw him go out the door for the hospital. He looked like he ordinarily did when he went to the hospital. He always looked the same. Dad never took the paraldehyde stuff; he'd been in bed since the Atlantic City trip, and Bill tapered him off. So he was a little nervous and shaky, but not any more than I'd seen him on a lot of other mornings when he'd go to the hospital. He just told Bill that was his last drink and he'd be back after the operation. I heard him say it. He said he was really going to do it.

Mom and Bill talked in the kitchen, and I guess I was fixing my hair and maybe went out for a little while since it was such a bright, warm day. I don't remember Mom starting to worry until lunch. We had lunch, and when Dad didn't come home by lunch time, she started getting a little anxious. I remember her pacing back and forth in the living room, watching out the window. You know, with an alcoholic you never relax. I mean, the old feeling comes back, and it did with her. She got that uneasiness.

Bill didn't get upset; he was busy calming Mom down. Then even he started to get a little worried after so long a time. But then Dad called and said he'd be home. When he came home, it turned out he was just out making restitution.

There wasn't any program then. The restitution idea was one of the things he got from the Oxford Group. Mom's notebook shows how much of A.A. came from there—restitution, surrendering, and so forth. Later on, they did the surrendering, for the new ones, right upstairs in Dad's room where it would be more private. And this was way before the Twelve Steps were ever written down.

June 10, 1935, was the birthdate of A.A., but I didn't see any big change, not right away. Dad was trying to get his practice back. He'd be gone to the hospital in the morning. Then he usually went to the city club for lunch and played cards for a while until his office hours. He'd have office hours from 2 to 4, and after 4 p.m. he'd usually come home. Then Bill would go downtown with him, or sometimes Bill would go over to Henrietta's with Mom and talk, or Dad and Bill would sit in the kitchen and talk. Bill was a talker—he would just take over the conversation. It didn't matter who he was with.

Finally, they were getting a little bit restless. They needed someone to work on. They got Eddie R., of course, and that was a little excitement. He was the first drunk they tried to fix. He was the one that shinnied down the drainpipe and chased Mom with the butcher knife.

When Eddie and his family came, I had to sleep on the davenport because they had two little kids and they all slept in my room. My room only had space for a small bed, a dresser, and a night table. Finally, they shipped Eddie's kids off to Grandma's or somewhere. Things weren't going too well, I guess. I'd see Eddie's wife come down with black eyes in the morning where he'd smacked her around a little. He wasn't a real good example, because he was their first attempt and it was a complete flop.

41

I understood why Eddie was there and what they were trying to do with him and why they were trying to do it. I understood the fact that they needed someone to work with because I'd heard them say it. But it wasn't anything they told me directly. I just lost my room and slept on the davenport.

I was all for this since it gave me a chance to see Ray more often. It was easier when they were all involved like that. They couldn't watch me as carefully. But they were heartbroken when Eddie didn't pan out. So they had to find another one. They felt so sure this thing would work. I'd hear them talking about it, hunched over the kitchen table at all hours. They thought people were just going to flock to it, but of course, it didn't work that way, and it still doesn't. They'd looked hard and long for Eddie, and then it turned out he was one of the ones who couldn't accept it. Also, he had an allergy to tuna which we didn't know about, so when Mom gave him the tuna sandwich, he went berserk. He chased her with a butcher knife. So they had to have somebody new for both of them to work on, to try their cure. Finally Dad got the idea of calling the hospital and that's when they got Bill D.

I remember Bill D. through this letter that was written after the following letter was written by Henrietta D., Bill D.'s wife, after Mom died. It was supposed to be part of a *Grapevine* article on Mom that never got published for whatever reason. Bill's wife wrote the letter to Bill W.:

"On Friday, June 28, 1935, I met Anne Smith . . . the most thoughtful, understanding person I have ever known. After talking to her awhile, I addressed her as Mrs. Smith and she said, 'Anne to you, my dear.' She wanted to remove all barriers. She wanted God to have full credit for this wonderful thing that happened to her. Bill W. was there at this time. After they talked with me for awhile, Anne asked me if I would like to 'go all the way with God.' I told her I would. She said we should kneel, which we all did, and told me to surrender myself to God and ask Him if He had a plan for me to reveal it to me.

"Anne taught me to have a 'quiet time' in the morning that I might feel near to God and receive strength for the day. She taught me to surrender my husband to God and not try to tell him how to stay sober, as I had tried that and failed. Anne taught me to love everyone.

She said 'Ask yourself, "What is wrong with me today if I don't love you?"' . . . She told me I should never criticize the remarks of the person leading the meeting as we do not know God's plan. Maybe what that person says will meet the need of someone in the group . . . In the early part of 1936, Anne organized a 'woman's group' for wives of alcoholics, whereby in her loving way, she tried to teach us patience, love, and unselfishness . . . Anne made it very plain to me from the beginning that she wanted no credit for herself, it was God. All she wanted was to keep herself so she could know and follow God's plan."

This letter shows what I mean about Mom being the Mother of A.A. and Al-Anon. Also, I feel that Dad helped Bill as much as Bill helped Dad at that time. Bill was the promoter, Mom was the stabilizer, and Dad was the rock. Dad had a lot of stability when it came to keeping a level head. Bill was always up and down. He'd sit in a chair all slouched over, and cigarette ashes would be all around. He was kind of a nervous wreck. He had ulcers. That's how the tomatoes, sauerkraut, and Karo syrup cure came to be. Bill thought sauerkraut cured everything. Anyone who came into A.A. at our house got slapped into bed and dosed with that stuff. Like Smitty says, those early ones had a rugged time.

When Dad got the idea of getting drunks to fix from the hospital, things kind of picked up. It changed my life in a way because it got to be more open. They had more people coming in. At first I'd just sit there and listen. Then gradually I knew them better and they drew me out a little. I could talk a little more. I was less bashful. I had to be.

You could see that Dad was quieting down, too. I think he finally could see the light at the end of the tunnel. When he went to Atlantic City, I don't really call that a slip because he had not accepted the program yet. There was no program. Dad and Mom and Bill were working out the program.

At that time I was getting involved with the quiet times they had in the morning. The guys would come, and Mom would have her quiet time with them. There was a cookie salesman and he'd bring the stale cookies over, and we'd take up a collection for three pounds of coffee for 29 cents. Then they'd have their quiet time, which is a holdover from the Oxford Group, where they read the Bible, prayed and listened, and got guidance. Then they'd have coffee and cookies. This was early in the morning, when the sky was just starting to get light. Sometimes they'd get us out of bed to do this.

Then there were the Oxford Group meetings that they went to at T. Henry and Clarace Williams' house. I went with Dad and Mom and Bill—but not too many, because those nights were my sure shots at seeing Ray. I had to be home to put the coffee on though.

I was more involved in my own life because I was always looking for a way to see Ray. It was a full-time job. We weren't playing ball out in the street at that time. We had one neighbor that was kind of squawking about it, so we had to drop the street games. When we wanted to play ball, we'd go up to the schoolyard and play in the evening.

It wasn't like we were by ourselves. We had groups. Mom and Dad knew Ray would be there, but they also knew we weren't going to be alone either. So I couldn't see what all the fuss was about. We weren't doing anything bad. We just needed to be together.

I never got to the place where I hated my Dad. You hate the actions, but the person, well, you love him. He and I were, I think, real close. And for him, that was something, because I don't think he gave too much of a damn about other kids. His kids were fine—up to a point. Let's face it, we weren't joys, but I think he still loved us a heck of a lot, though there were times when you wondered if he did or not.

I don't think my dad wanted me to marry anybody. I don't think he would have ever thought anybody was good enough for me. I told Ray, "I bet you thought you were getting the Hope Diamond, didn't you?"

In the autumn of 1935, when Dad and Bill started A.A., although it didn't have a name then, I first met Ernie. I met him through A.A. I guess it was supposed to be that way. The Lord has more than one way to get you down on your knees, you know. He didn't hit me with the bottle. He hit me with Ernie.

5
ERNIE

When I first saw Ernie, he stopped me on the street. I was walking home from the bus stop, carrying my school books. Of course, I never took the West Exchange Street bus to go home; I always took the West Market Street bus that went by Ray's house. Ernie stopped and asked where Dr. Smith lived. I just kept on walking and said, "Right down there." I didn't tell him that I was Sue Smith. After he drove down there I walked up, and there I was.

He had heard about Dad from his parents. They were very religious and were members of the same church as the Williamses. They found out about Dad through the Williamses and the Oxford Group. They heard about this doctor that could help drunks get sober.

At that time, Ernie said he was 30. He must have been a little older, because when he went to collect his Social Security they found out he was a year older. But at the time, we thought he was only 30. He was the first young person they had to try their cure on. But Ernie had double trouble. I call him industrial-strength trouble. Ernie was divorced for the second time, and he had a kid, Ernie, Jr., no job, and he wanted to get sober.

I was about 17. In fact, Ernie Jr. was only a few years younger than me. I didn't pay any attention to Ernie. I didn't like him. I thought he was a smarty, you know. He was stout, with reddish hair and a round face with blue eyes. He was outgoing, the life-of-the-party type. Ernie was single then and he kept coming to the house, and I think my dad got the bright idea that if he could get Ernie to take me out, and he'd pay the way, he might be able to get me away from Ray. We'd go down and get hamburgers, and Dad would buy them. I knew all that, but I didn't realize it was in connection with Ray at the time. Now I think it was. I think Dad was using Ernie, and it backfired on him.

Then Ray got a job out of town, and my girlfriend got married and moved out of town. So I was more or less stuck at home with the new A.A.'s coming in, which weren't too many at the time. And there was the Depression, so people couldn't afford to do much except entertain each other. Ernie and I just got thrown together. He'd come over to the house and we'd go out and get a hamburger for a dime, or something like that. At first, he was just somebody to pass the time with. That's what people did then, sat on the porch and passed time.

In 1936, when Ray first went away, I used to write to him, and of course my dad objected. This was when he was in the Civilian Conservation Corps camp, in Likely, California. "The coldest spot on earth," Ray called it. When he wrote, he would always draw a picture on the envelope instead of his name and address.

Well, my dad caught on and kind of tried to stop that, so I wrote Ray and told him to send my letters over to his house and I'd pick them up there. One day, I went downtown with my dad and we went by the apartment where Ray lived. There was the mailman delivering the mail, and my dad stopped and picked up the letters for me. So I knew I was shot. My dad wasn't a dummy. That's what I used to tell my kids, "You don't need to try to pull anything over on me; I think I've done it all." I did most of it, anyway.

Ernie gradually started to have some appeal. He was an older person and he had a good sense of humor. We always had fun. We joked together. He was a real storyteller. He could make my mom and dad laugh like nobody I've ever seen, just sitting around the kitchen table, telling stories, and drinking coffee. Like I say, they were pushing me, so I figured they liked him. And that was kind of different.

For a couple of years I was seeing Ernie just because he was here. He was a good time, that's all. Then Ray would come back in town for a weekend and I would sneak out to see him whenever I could. I needed to see him. But I wasn't fooling Dad. You'd be surprised how many times we would be out and Dad would be there. One time we walked up this one street, a little alley or whatever you call it, with snapdragons and hollyhocks growing along the sides. We figured nobody would ever come up this way. So we walked up there and, would you believe, my dad's car was sitting there? I've often wondered what in the hell he was doing there. He came up by us and took us home. He never said a word about it. I can't imagine why he was there. He was sober then, too.

Ray bought me a ring on one of those trips when he came back for Christmas. I snuck out to see him and met him up at the schoolyard. It was cold and windy. When he gave it to me, he tried to put it on my finger, and I said, "You know I can't wear it." There was no way I could wear it without getting shot. So I put it away in a drawer and finally, after I could see that things weren't going right, I took it back to his house one time when I knew he wasn't there. I gave it to his mother. She just looked at me real hard and shook her head. She knew what it meant.

I even asked him to get married one time, and he turned me down. He said it was because he didn't have a job, and because he knew how Mom and Dad felt toward him. But I think if he'd had a job, he would have done it.

Then one time, in the fall of 1937, I went out with Ray, and when I came home Ernie was at the house. I tried to go upstairs without being noticed, but he cornered me in the hall and asked me if I'd been out with Ray. I looked him straight in the eyes and I said "yes." So, by gosh, if he didn't whip up and grab me by the arm and get me in the car and drive over to Ray's apartment. Ray was hanging out on the corner, as usual, with a bunch of the guys. It was a warm night. Ernie got Ray in the car and that was when I broke up with Ray. Ernie just told Ray that Dad didn't want me to see him, and I don't remember what the thing was—whether I had to make up my mind or whatever. I don't remember. I didn't say much. I couldn't even look at Ray. Ray says he got the impression that Ernie was taking over and that he was out. But I know for about three weeks I wasn't worth a nickel around there, burning the toast and forgetting to put the coffee on. I was grouchy and mean because I had broken up with Ray. I didn't really want to, but I was beginning to like Ernie then, too. Ray said he never cried in his life, but he did that night.

I had graduated from high school in 1936. I had to take an extra half-year because I wasn't the best in geometry, and I hated history and wasn't the best in that either. I was so shy in school that even if I knew the answer when I was called upon, I wouldn't say it. I used to say, "I don't know." So I didn't graduate with Smitty's class. I graduated in June of that year. He graduated in the January class.

It was the Depression in '36, and they had a WPA school. You could go there and learn typing and shorthand. Then I went to business college. I got to go for free because Dad sobered up the brother-in-law of the man who owned the school. Otherwise I'd never have been able to go there.

I was seeing Ernie, and Dad was starting to be against that. The more he was against it, the more I stuck up for it. I thought, what the hell, they aren't going to like anybody.

I don't think anybody would have suited Dad. I was his girl. He'd have been happy to keep me at home. Any male that I picked up with, Dad did not cotton to for very long.

Ernie wasn't the nicest person. I already knew he was a womanizer. When I went to the WPA school, sometimes he'd take a friend of mine home, usually Barb or Vianna. Barb told me she'd go out to the car and there was this gal waiting in the car. And he'd act like this gal wasn't there. He wouldn't introduce her or anything. I don't know how many times he left people sitting in the car while he went visiting somewhere. He was going with a zillion girls at the same time. He was like Will Rogers—he never met a woman he didn't like.

Ernie had a lot of appeal, though. Too much appeal. He appealed to everybody. Like my girlfriend Elgie would say, "I don't know what it was. It just seems like you were fascinated with that guy." And that was it. He surprised me and brought me presents, candy, and flowers. I liked that. When I was with him, I felt like I was the number one girl. Then I'd hear about him and some other gal, or he wouldn't show up, and I'd just bawl. Then he'd show up with a box of candy and I'd think he'd changed. You always think they're gonna change. After a while, you can't give it up.

He did stay sober at first. He was A.A. number four. That's how he got into the Big Book, the first one. He was dropped in the second edition because he started drinking again. He was boozing by the time we were married. That was one reason Dad didn't like him. The other, of course, is that Ernie double-crossed him. I've heard people say Dad always thought Ernie was an S.O.B.; he was the only person Dad was ever heard to talk about like that.

Dad got along with everyone. Bill didn't, but Dad did. Dad was busy with the program then, and he was trying to get back his medical practice, too. He was treating the A.A.s for free. It seemed like staying sober took as much of him as the drinking had before that.

Then they started working on the Big Book, and I saw some of the stories being written at our dining room table. It must have been 1938 or so. There was quite a bit of argument about that, too, as I recall. I typed some of them up myself at the business college.

I wasn't much involved at the time, but I remember when they broke away from the Oxford Group in 1939. Dad was so upset about it he had to go to bed for a day or so. I was over at Elgie's place just a few days ago, and Johnny was talking about that night. He was there when they split. He said Dad and Mom left the Oxford Group that night after Clarence S. announced they were going to have a special meeting just for the alcoholics.

Dad and Mom went out the door first, and Johnny says he was right behind them. Henrietta Seiberling was behind him, and she was yelling at Dad, saying, "That's a terrible thing you've done! You'll live to regret this! Dr. Smith, you shouldn't do that!" Finally, she kept blowing off, and Johnny turned around and said, "Henrietta, for God's sake, shut your mouth!" And she glared at him. So I know it must have been rough on Dad. He was pretty sensitive about people whenever there was loyalty involved. My dad was loyal, and he taught that to me. I am loyal, that's one thing I can say.

Dad and I got along pretty good until this thing with Ernie came along. I got in an argument with my dad one night because he raised cain with me about Ernie, and he said, "You might just as well marry Ray." And I said, "Well, why don't you make up your mind?" He grabbed me. He would grab me by the arm and dig those fingernails into me. And he'd give me that look. But this time I just gave it right back. I'd just as soon he slug me and get it over with, you know.

But it seemed like I couldn't win. I don't think I picked out kids that were bad, but it just seemed like everybody I picked out as a friend, they objected to. That's why I left home. We were arguing about Ernie. There was that hard edge in Dad's voice. It cut a big, empty place inside me. I just decided, well, before we hate each other's guts, I might as well take off.

So, I saw an ad in the paper one day, and I went up on North Hill and rented a room. I had a job that I had gotten through an A.A. I got sixteen bucks a week, and I had to pay seven for the room. But that was all right. I wasn't going anywhere.

I didn't move in right away. Dad didn't even know that I had the place. One time we were arguing and I just told them, "Well, I'm going to move out." It was January 1941. I was 22. And I had lived at home for 17 years.

They were kind of surprised I already had a room. They tried to talk me out of it. Even Elgie, Johnny R.'s wife, came over and spent about an hour talking to me in my room. But my mind was made up; I already had the key in my pocket. I'd had it for weeks. Heck, I was going to be 23 in February. Smitty had left for the Army already.

It was cold as all get out. Dad helped me move. I took my little record player. I had some records, and my clothes. I didn't have a great deal. Dad drove me over, helped me carry my stuff from the car to inside the door, but he wouldn't go up to the room. I carried everything up myself.

And as my dad was getting into the car, the wind whipping at his coat, he said, "Just remember, young lady, wherever you go, you take yourself with you." Like I say, he could give you that old Vermont chill. I didn't see or talk to them for a few months, except Dad did call once to tell me the *Saturday Evening Post* article on A.A. was out. That was their big break-through. It changed their lives.

I don't think I went home until Mother's Day. When I came to the door, Dad got tears in his eyes, and he said, "What took you so long?" So I knew that I'd upset him real badly. But I couldn't let Mother's Day go by without taking Mom something. So I did, and then we started speaking again. Dad would call me once in a while, and sometimes we'd run into each other on the street downtown. Then, when I got married, we lost contact again.

6

THE LEGACY OF THE DISEASE

Ernie and I were married in September of 1941. I was 23. He was 37. I'd
been gone from home about five or six months. The only people that were
at the wedding were my mother-in-law and father-in-law. They were the
only two besides the minister in a little church up in Cuyahoga Falls.

Ernie was drunk when we got married. He'd stepped off the wagon—
again. He'd lost part of his little finger in an accident with a water pump and
started drinking for the pain. He was boozing it up the night we were
married. The night was warm, and I was wearing a green dress made of some
new fabric that was too heavy. I had a big corsage my mother-in-law must
have picked out, but it didn't match.

After the wedding, I was out of town for nine months, in Lodi. We
were so broke I think I gave Mom and Dad handkerchiefs for Christmas.
Talk about living in a dump, we did it. There was a big, high, windy hill and
an empty house. We lived in one room of that house, and it was cold and
miserable. After a few months, we got a place uptown and went to two
rooms with yellow curtains.

I think I was in love with him at the time. We had some good times.
We kidded with each other. My step-daughter-in-law, Ginny, told me not
too long ago, "Ernie Jr. and I used to get the biggest kick out of you two."

She says, "The way you two used to sit and joke back and forth with each other, it just tickled the death out of us." And we did have fun that way.

Ernie would buy me clothes. He'd surprise me with flowers or candy or something. And later, he'd try to help with the kids. But I really didn't realize how much he was running around. Nobody ever told me until afterward.

As I said, I think I was in love with him at the time. I thought he'd straighten up. Of course, you always think you're going to straighten them up. He had fallen off before and come back out of it, and I kept thinking he would again. Eventually he did, for about 11 years. Then we went to St. Louis. It was in 1955, when A.A. came of age. He started drinking again. He was chasing around, too. I'd find letters from women. I think I could have taken just the boozing, but I couldn't take both of them. After 24 years, I just said, the hell with it, and got divorced. I'm a slow learner.

You know it's said, "Stay together for the kids." That's a crock. I stayed because of lack of confidence. If I'd have thought I could have gone out and made a good living with those kids, I think I would have gone. But I just didn't have the confidence. Maybe he saw to it. Maybe he kept me that way.

There were times when Ernie was real good to me and times when he was critical as hell. He would call it constructive criticism, but I call it destructive. He used to say he taught me how to dress and what to think. Well, he did do that. Shy and introverted is what I was, and he made me more so, like I was nothing without him.

His own son, Ernie Jr., from his first marriage, says, "I don't know why you ever stuck it out with him." Ernie Jr. is just a few years younger than me, and we've always been good friends. In fact, in some ways I'm still closer to him and his wife, Ginny, than I was to Ernie.

Ernie was a salesman. He sold cars. He sold industrial roofing and asphalt. He was in the service for a while. I don't know whether he was really a good salesman or not. I think he just out-sat people. They had to fight to get rid of him.

He was drunk for quite a while after we were married. He was mean and would yell at the top of his voice if you dared cross him in any way. He got a little nasty. I've been smacked a few times. So, one of the last times he smacked me, I picked up a cup and wheeled it at him, and I put a gash in his leg.

He kept drinking until '46 or so. The only reason he quit was the doctor thought he had a heart condition, and it scared him to death. I don't think he ever had a heart condition. I don't think he had a heart.

We moved in September 1945, about three weeks before my daughter, Bonna Lee, was born. It was a nice neighborhood then, and we bought the best house we could afford. We didn't have hardly anything to move. We had a bed, and that was about it. We did some work in the kitchen. After that we didn't have anything left to fix up the house with. We didn't have anything until Mom and Dad died and we brought some of their stuff here.

That first Christmas, Ernie was drinking. Mickey, my son, was 20 months old, and Bonna was just a couple of months. My in-laws called me and wanted me to come down to their house for Christmas, because that's where Ernie was. And I said, "No way. I'm staying in my own home for Christmas." So they dragged Ernie back up there for Christmas.

They had to come up. They had to bring him up, even though I'd have been just as happy if they'd stayed away. My mother-in-law said, "Well, he's got a lovely present for you." She told me what it was. And I said, "You know, there's other things more important than that. I'd rather have a little peace of mind from him." She was a big woman, and she looked down at me and said, "Well, now you just have to be more understanding."

I didn't get too much sympathy from Mom and Dad, and I didn't expect to, either. I never told them we were married. They must have heard about it or read the notice in the paper. I think they thought that Ernie had double-crossed them, which he did. Then, too, we lived out in Lodi for nine months after we were married, so we weren't close by. We did come into town to go to meetings once in a while, but usually I stayed out there, and he got a job working nights. So I didn't see Mom and Dad.

I know why they didn't try to see me. They were hurt. At that time, in their will, they had cut me down to $1. Later they put me back in, but what I did get out of Dad's estate got blown as part of our trucking business, and that was the end of it.

We really didn't have a whole lot to do with each other until I heard indirectly that Mother had broken her ankle. I called her then and asked if I could do anything, or come over and fix her meals or something. It was Pearl Harbor Day, December 7, 1941, and we were in Akron. When we got back to

Lodi, the guy that we left the station with had disappeared with all the money. There wasn't a whole lot, but it was all there was. I think it was then that I called Mom. It seemed like from then on we at least got along agreeably.

So I did get together with Mom and Dad again, but they didn't get involved in my life much. Like when the kids were born, I don't think it was any occasion for them. I don't remember them calling or sending flowers, or coming to the hospital or anything. The in-laws were there. One time they got real upset because I didn't let my mother-in-law take care of me when Bonna was born. With Mickey, we were living with them, so I didn't have much choice. Every time that baby yelled they picked him up. They spoiled him rotten.

Mom and Dad stayed out of it. Neither one of them ever said anything about the way Ernie really was or anything. But my dad would talk to other people about him. I hear Dad grew a healthy dislike for him. And Bill—well, Bill came down one time when Ernie and I were still together, and Bill and I made this tape about A.A. and Dad. But on that tape, Ernie said something to Bill and Bill shot back at him, "I gave up on you a long time ago, you son of a bitch!" That's right on the tape.

I really didn't talk to my dad about Ernie. I talked to my mother more than I did him. When I was having my troubles, I'd go over there and sit in the kitchen, and Mom would say, "You wouldn't be happy without Ernie." I often wonder if she really meant that or if she was afraid she was going to get me back. But that's what she used to tell me. You know, put up and shut up. The kids were real little then. Mom and Dad really didn't get to know Bonna too well. Bonna was born in '45 and Mother died in '49.

Then, too, they were pretty active in the groups. They would go to Cleveland and Toledo. They went to Florida. With two kids at home, I didn't get very far away. I didn't have a car then. But we did get along. I understood that they had a new life, and to me that was very acceptable. Because they had that other kind of life for so damned long.

After a while, when they were home, Dad would stop by here on his way to the hospital in the mornings. He stopped by a lot of times, and he'd have a cup of coffee and stay a half-hour or so. Maybe every other morning, whenever it hit him. I think he enjoyed those visits. I know I did.

I lived with Mom and Dad for ten days or two weeks one time when

I had agoraphobia. That was when Mom took me shopping. The agoraphobia started at a funeral, in 1947 or '48.

When you have agoraphobia, you're afraid to go out. You just don't know what's going to happen to you. I could hardly go to the front door. Of course Ernie's solution for that was a little shot of whiskey. Well, I didn't like whiskey. But I needed something, because I couldn't leave the house. I couldn't go out to see Mom and Dad. Sometimes I could get over there if someone would take me, but not by myself. I was scared to death.

One time, Bill was at the house, and Dad and Mom told him about it. I had gone over there to spend a week or two because I was having such a bad time. Mom decided to take me shopping, because that is what you did in those days. When you felt bad, you went out and got a new pair of shoes or a hat or something. Well, I just about had a fit. I'd just as soon go around the house naked as go downtown. I was that scared.

Bill came up to the house and talked to me. He said, You know, Susie, what normal people do when something is bothering them is jump in the haymow with someone new. But that never solves anything, and hell, I had enough trouble jumping in with the same old guy. Like Bill said, it's easy to run away from a problem; it's a lot harder to face it. So we talked about it. I imagine he talked to me just about like he talked to my dad back when they met in 1935.

Bill spent three or four hours with me. Then he said, "Well, Susie, let's start to work on the hexes." And he said, "Let's take a walk." I said, "I don't think so, Bill." And he said, "Yeah, we're gonna take a walk up to the corner."

So we went up the block and back. I finally got back home, and I about passed out. Then 20 minutes later, he said, "Okay, Susie, now you can go up by yourself." I said, "I'll never make it, Bill." He said, "Yeah, you'll make it." So I could see I wasn't going to get out of it. That was one of the worst days of my life, or maybe, in another way, it was one of the best.

Later, shortly after Dad died, we went up to New York to see Bill and Lois. I remember we helped Bill chop down a tree. That was the trip when I asked Bill to get in touch with Dr. Norman Vincent Peale for me, up there in New York, because I'd heard he could help me. So he did, and Dr. Peale told Bill that since I was from Akron, it would be better if I just went to see Dr. McKay, a local Akron minister. Dr. Peale said, he's one of our men, and he's very good. So I did go, and he was very helpful.

There was another doctor, one of Ernie's friends. She gave me some kind of pill. Then I found out that it wasn't so good. If I got real bad, I took it. If I didn't, I didn't have to take it. If I stayed home, I didn't take anything.

Then I decided to try going out on my own. I stopped the pills, and I just forced myself to try to do what I could. I gradually got to where I could go out in a car. We started out by driving around to look at the leaves in the fall. I could drive somewhere, after that. As long as I had that car close to me and knew that if I got that panicky feeling I could get in the car and get home, I was all right.

But I still don't do much walking. Seems like when I'd look down a distance it would seem so far, like looking down the railroad tracks. I get that panicky feeling, and so I don't walk too much.

I did do a lot of praying and a lot of reading. I read a little book when I was staying up there on Ardmore Avenue, a book my dad gave me. I got a lot of comfort out of it. It's called *Life Abundant for You*. I would read it by the hour. Sometimes I still look at it.

I really didn't talk to Dad or Mom about Ernie, or about my in-laws and the trouble I had with the kids. That's another thing. The minute my kids were born, I became a complete moron overnight. I didn't know anything about raising kids. But I figured it was my kid to learn with. My in-laws didn't agree. They just kept at me all the time, saying I wasn't doing anything right. And Ernie would agree with them. I had a hell of a time.

I was scared to death to have a kid. I was scared of the physical part, the birth, and scared of being a mother, too. I didn't know what to do. I wonder if I'm sort of like my dad on that. I thought that kids were fine for the neighbors.

My in-laws made me feel like a moron, too. They would give me books on immaturity. And if I wanted to do something with the kids a certain way, they would say, "You shouldn't do it that way." They wanted me to do it their way. They wanted me to rock the kids whenever they wanted it, and pick them up whenever they screamed. Spoil 'em, as I call it. And of course I never did keep house the way they wanted. I didn't go over

Mickey and Bonna as toddlers.

Bonna and Mickey.

and visit them like you would when you get along with people, and they noticed that. I resented them and so I threw up a mental block. They would come in the front door and I would go out the back door.

My in-laws would have kept the kids all the time if I'd let 'em. And they would have spoiled them rotten, too. When Mickey was a baby we lived with them, so every time he yelled he got picked up. He was born April 3, 1944, so that summer I rented a cottage out on the lake. It belonged to Dr. Tunks. I took that kid out there and I let him scream his guts out. I didn't care.

I'd go out on the porch or down by the lake or somewhere and just let him yell. I wasn't going to spoil him. He only slept about four hours a night. We used to call him "Edison." He was a hard kid.

Then Bonna came along when Mickey was about 18 months old. I let her scream, too. Once I probably let her scream when I shouldn't. It turned out she was having a problem with her bowels. I really shouldn't have let her cry, but I did. But you know, my daughter was a different person, she was always different from day one.

Since my in-laws were always interfering, I didn't think I could go to them with questions about the kids. Because I figured if I asked them anything I'd just get told I was an idiot again. They didn't actually tell me I was, but they sure acted like I was. And I didn't ask my mom or dad. I really felt they were uncomfortable with the kids. We would go over there, and Mom had this one metal dog and the kids could play with that. I thought that was one of the things they shouldn't play with—it had thin legs and it looked like it would break easily. But that was the only thing they could play with, and eventually it did break.

7

Putting Up the Block

Mom didn't really have much time with the kids. She died on June 1, 1949, before Bonna was four years old. She wasn't well. When I was in high school, she had gotten to the place where she couldn't drive. She started losing her sight when we were young. That was one of the reasons I always did the housework for her, anything I could do to help out. When she died, she was almost blind.

Mom and Dad were coming back from a visit to Smitty's in May of '49, and it was raining really hard. They had to walk in the rain from one plane to another at O'Hare Airport in Chicago, and Mom evidently caught a cold. We picked them up in the airport in Cleveland, and she was not well, with her heart trouble and a cold. During the night, Dad had to take her to the hospital.

She was conscious for a few days, but she just didn't fight it. I kind of think she gave up, because she knew about Dad's cancer and she didn't want to be left alone. She wasn't in a coma when she went in, but she slipped into a coma about two or three days before she died.

Dad was staying there with her. He had a room at one end, and she was at the other. I was there most of the time. The night she died, Dad and I were there with her, just the two of us. It was real quiet. When she went, he looked at me and said, "Well, Susie, we just lost a good friend." He was lost. He was really lost.

You know, she pulled him through. She was his rock. After she died, everyone was pulling at him about where to bury her. Some wanted her buried one place, and others wanted her at another place. Smitty and I told him he had to stick up for his own decision. So he finally put her where he wanted her. But after that, it seemed like he was always lost.

He had some help, Emma and LaVelle, and they took care of him over at the house. And I went over whenever I could. I could see he was failing. Finally, he was in the hospital. The kids were little, but I could get over there in the morning because Ernie could watch Bonna, and Mickey was in kindergarten.

The day he died, I went to the hospital in the morning. It was very warm for November, but I had gotten a new coat, so I went over to see him and to show off my coat. I said, "Boy, what a day for it! It's so hot!" And he said, "Don't worry about it, you'll need it."

I got home from the hospital around noon. Ernie left, and Mickey came home. It was after I fed them lunch that the hospital called and wanted me to come right away.

So, I called my mother-in-law and asked her if she would take care of the kids. I told her I'd bring them over, but I didn't have a car. So I called one of our workmen from the business, and he came over and took the three of us to my mother-in-law's in a truck. I left the kids there and then I went over to the hospital. It all seemed to take so long, but I finally got there.

I went into the room. I was standing there alone a minute, looking at him, and he was dead. And I stood there. Then after a while this man came in and said we'd go down the hall. He took me down the hall but I don't remember what he told me. It was something about how he had wanted to catch me before I went in the room, and how Dad's heart had given out, and Dad had told the nurse, "Better call the family." The man with me wasn't even his doctor; it was just somebody who worked there.

I said, "Well, it's done." It was November 16, 1950. I don't remember how I got home. Then I was talking to somebody who called on the phone, and I think Ernie came home, and I put down the phone. I forgot all about them being on the phone. Then we went and made the arrangements.

Dr. Bob, near death, alone after Anne died.
Photograph taken in living room at 855 Ardmore Avenue.

We called Smitty, and he and his wife Betty came up. Betty didn't come up for Mother, but she came up with Smitty for Dad.

Smitty and Ernie and I planned the funeral. It was a long, drawn-out deal, too. We had visiting hours—I think it was Saturday, Sunday, and then Monday. It was a long time. And it was crowded. It was really crowded. Bill and Lois came down from New York.

On Monday, we went to the church where the services were done by Dr. Tunks. Then we just left, because Dad was being cremated and they took him from there. Mickey was only six when Dad died. The kids didn't go to the funeral. I can't see taking kids five and six years old to a funeral home.

They had a mammoth crowd all the time down there at the house and at the church. It was a trying time, really, with all the people there. I often think what it would be like today. There would be lines miles long.

It was probably just as well that Mother went first, because I don't know how she would have been able to stand it if he had gone first. We don't know and never will.

The Thursday after the funeral was Thanksgiving, and it was warm again. Then Friday we had a blizzard. In between the funeral and Thanksgiving we were over at the house, figuring out what we wanted. I told Smitty, "Now listen, there's nothing in the house that I want that's worth causing a breakup. There's not a thing here that I want that would cause that." He felt the same way, and we never had a squabble about it.

I don't know how I got through it—first Mom, then Dad died. All in a year. Maybe I just had to put up a mental block or lose my mind. I think I have a built-in block for things that I sense are wrong or bother me. Even today, if something really bugs me, I don't let it clutter my mind, because I've got enough problems without added ones.

That's how I get through things, I guess. I absorb so much, and I try to make peace with myself about it, and if I can't, then the old block goes up, and the hell with it. My mother always said if you have a problem that you can't solve, you should surrender it. Well, maybe I should try surrender instead of blocking it.

After Mom and Dad died, I went on trying to raise the kids, trying not to get mad at Ernie, and trying to put up with the in-laws. I didn't have much help. I didn't have anything, really. I didn't have the confidence to get a job. But I'd have been better off to go scratch with the chickens, if I'd known what I know now.

I think what made it hard for me with my kids was that constant opposition from Ernie—yes-and-no, no-and-yes. Whatever I said, Ernie would oppose it, regardless of what it was. So, of course, the kids would always go to Ernie. I never got things my way. They knew that whenever I said no, their dad would say yes. So they just went back and forth, and they always got their way. It made me feel crazy. It was easy for Ernie to come in and be lovey-dovey with the kids since he wasn't there all the time. He was away from home a lot, you know.

During one of his absences, when the kids were real little, we all got terrific headaches. I had a baby-sitter here one day, and when I came home she said, "I thought I smelled gas, so I called the gas company." She said they came right out and said, "You were lucky you didn't all die." We had to have the chimney cleaned out. It turned out the carbon monoxide was giving us all headaches. But Ernie was away from all that. We all could have died, and he wasn't there.

His family wasn't helping. And Ernie wasn't helping. He was either boozing or running around. Then he would breeze in and take the kids places. They'd think he was just great. But it was just an excuse. He would take them over and leave them at his mother's and go somewhere else, with some other gals.

By the time the kids hit junior high school, around 1957, he was heavy into boozing again. He started after we went to the second A.A. International in St. Louis in 1955. Bill called all of us, and Bill and Lois and Henrietta D. and Ernie and I flew out together. We met Smitty and Betty out there.

That evening they had a kind of social hour before dinner. They had a table of drinks at one end and soft drinks for the drunks at the other. We had a little meeting where we all sat around the table, and all the trustees of the New York Foundation were there. They started around the table, and everyone was supposed to say something. But not me; I couldn't do it.

After that conference I didn't have much A.A. contact. You know how hard it is to get out when you have kids. And I was still bothered by that agoraphobia. I went through quite a time there for a while. I think I could have put up with the boozing. But with this constant fighting over the kids and the other women and the boozing, I couldn't see where I was ever going to make out with any sanity. I was stuck with two kids and no confidence.

I didn't go back to my quiet times. I probably would have been better off if I'd done that. I never went to an Al-Anon meeting, either. I went to all of my Al-Anon meetings in 1935, when my mother started having special meetings for the families. I think I already had all the things you're supposed to have in Al-Anon. I think in a way I had tough love at that time. When the guy came to the door to deliver a case of booze to Ernie, I just said, "Bring it all in, bring in as much as you can—it's his choice."

The kids always knew when things were bad, because I'd put on Clyde McCoy's "Sugar Blues"—that was my favorite song—and I'd play it over and over. I played that thing to death. I did lots of things to try and feel better. I was a coffee drinker, smoker, shopper. I painted around the house. I did things with the kids. I would crochet and paint by numbers. When the kids were older, I took them to football and baseball games. Ernie went a few times—drunk—and embarrassed the hell out of the kids.

With his family always treating me like I was a nut, and Ernie always telling the kids yes when I said no, I just gave up with the kids. I told them to forget me, that I was just the middleman. They were going to do what they wanted anyhow. I'd get angry, but I could see it was no use. I did a lot of crying in those days.

Finally, sometime in early '62, I decided, "Boy, if I'm nuts, the best in the country's gonna tell me." So I called up Menninger's, and I went out there and found out I wasn't all that nuts.

Ernie came up with me, and he talked to them, too. But he left in a huff over something I told them up there. He said I was going to have to come crawling up the driveway to my kids before he'd let me come back. He said he was going to give me enough money to get an education to support myself and then I was going to be out on my own.

After he left, the doctors up there told me, "Just to set your mind straight, you aren't nuts, but your husband's got a few problems, and one of them is he has an abnormal relationship with his daughter."

I guess what they were talking about were some things that happened after we'd had fights and Ernie had been boozing. I know one time I took off

Sue, Mickey, and Ernie at a family gathering. The gestures and poses suggest something of the family dynamics at the time.

when he was boozing. This was one of the times I got smacked around, and left for a few days. My face was pretty beat up, so Bonna came over to where I was staying and went with me to the doctor.

That was when she told me that when he was drinking, he would have her sleep with him and all that. I told her, "You don't have to do that." "Well," she said, "then I get hit." I said, "Well, if you do, then we'll do something about it." I said, "Next time, if there's any problem, you just call your grandmother or me and we'll come and get you." Now don't get me wrong, he never really did anything. He was too drunk. But I guess that's what they meant by abnormal. She was always the apple of his eye, that sort of thing. He was always too drunk to really do anything.

But when I came back, I didn't have to crawl up the driveway like he said. In fact, he came running up to Menninger's to get me. Because that was when we found out Bonna was pregnant. Sixteen years old, and pregnant.

8
BONNA

Bonna was always different. I wasn't comfortable with her when she was little. She was competitive, even when she was a little baby. She always seemed like she had to be ahead. If she'd be crawling and Mickey would be ahead of her, she'd paw at him, and he was a year and a half older. If you played cards with her, she'd get mad if you beat her. You had to let her win. There was just no living with her if you beat her at cards. Even up 'til she was 10 years old, she was that way about cards. The neighbor lady next door called Bonna incorrigible. She was just a funny kid.

When we were down in Alabama once, when Ernie was working a job down there, Bonna fell down some steps and I often wondered if that affected her in some way. She was a young baby then, maybe a year old or a little older.

I used to watch her when we'd go downtown. I would carry my purse, and I bought her a little purse to carry. I got to watching her, and she would be watching me with my purse. I would take my purse and I would change it to the other arm, and pretty soon she would take her purse and change it to her other arm.

We were at the grocery store another time, and there was a cellar stairway. I didn't even see it and she just tumbled down. The guy just about had a fit. I often wondered if that also might have done something to her.

I had all kinds of trouble being a mother. There were times I just didn't know what to do. I couldn't keep my little girl in bed. I tried everything I knew. I'd leave the light on and leave the door open, and this, that, and the other. Finally—this would probably be child abuse today—I tied her leg to the bed for about a week. She would scream and carry on, but I still tied her in there. Finally, she got the message. I always felt kind of guilty about that. But I didn't know what else I could do. I've often wondered if some of her resentment toward me maybe stemmed from that.

Then one time, my stepson, Ernie Jr., and his wife Ginny were up here. It was Mickey's bedtime, time to say good night, and he wouldn't say good night. So he and I had a 15-minute shouting session. I would say, "Say good night!" And he'd be yelling, "No!" He was crying, and Ginny and Ernie Jr., said, "Oh, forget it." And I said, "No, I'm not going to forget it." Bonna was in the other room. She was yelling, "Good night! Good night!" the whole time.

Things like that were funny, but sometimes I think maybe I was too much like my Dad. I mean he wanted you to mind him and that was it. He wanted control, and he didn't want any argument about it.

Maybe I was a little too strict, but then Ernie was too-permissive. We'd start arguments about the kids. Ernie said I treated the dogs nicer than I treated the kids. I said, "Why in the hell should I beat the dog? He didn't do anything to me. Why should I beat the dog?"

I think I was more like my dad. So was Smitty. Once when Smitty and Betty were visiting, Smitty was trying to correct their kids—and Betty jumped on him about it. And he said, "Well, doggone, I want them to do this and I want them to do that." She said, "Yeah, but you don't have to treat them like they're bad."

I'm sure there were a lot of times, as I look back on it, that I did a lot of things I shouldn't have. I think maybe everybody tries to put an older head on a young kid. It doesn't work. No way. They're like my kitten. It doesn't know it's not supposed to go in the house when the door's open, because I've taken it in there before to get it food. So now, when I open the door, it's conditioned to sneak in if it can. Kids get the same way. They have built-in want-to's. But that doesn't make them bad. That wasn't always clear to me back then. There's so much more that you understand about kids today than we did back then.

I tried to lead them for so long. Then after a while, it was impossible, so instead of the kid giving up, the mother gave up. I just put up the old block. I think I would have been a lot better off, and I think my kids would have been better off, if I had left.

Bonna was the kind of child that always had to be the leader. In fact, they called me from camp one day. We used to send the kids to summer camp because I had to help Ernie with the business. In the summer, camp was the best place. It was a day camp; they were home morning and night. They left about 8:30 or 9, and then I'd go to work and I'd be back home by the time they got back home. They loved it.

But this one time, the guy that owned the camp called and said, "Hey, Bonna isn't exactly what we want up here. We'd appreciate it if you'd keep her home." She was only 12 or 13 then, and she was already a good-looking girl. And I asked him, "What's the problem?" Like I didn't know it already. I knew. She was a leader, but she was a leader in the wrong way. She was leading them into evil, or I guess you would say trouble. They didn't have to tell me what she was doing. That was enough for me. I just told Ernie, "Well, they don't want her at camp anymore."

She would try her darnedest to get a ribbon or something when she was horseback riding. She never got one. But old Mick, he never gave a damn, and he got 'em. They'd have been better off separated, I think. She was always just the opposite of Mickey.

She was the kind of kid who would cry her eyes out for something 'til she got it, then toss it aside. When she'd want to borrow one of her girlfriend's sweaters, she'd keep at her and keep at her 'til she got it, and then she wouldn't even wear the darned thing. Like she never could get enough. She had to be first, but then it was never enough.

I don't know why she was so driven to be number one. I tried not to give her too much attention, but I did try to give her enough attention.

I tried not to make it so that Mickey felt cheated. I tried not to spoil them. Like I say, I sure screwed up somewhere. I feel like I did, anyhow. It seemed like the whole bunch of them were working against me. I couldn't win.

Bonna always made me uncomfortable. But she always knew she could get away with anything with her father. Maybe there was something there I didn't know about and didn't realize.

Right before I went to Menninger's, we found Bonna on the floor one night. She had passed out. Ernie found her, and woke me up and said, "Something's the matter with Bonna. I gave her a tranquilizer to calm her down. We should call an ambulance." So we did, and took her over there to the hospital. She was rolling around in pain. Turns out she had an ovarian cyst that burst, and they operated on her right away.

I was over there every day and evening. I stayed with her constantly. The doctor finally told me I was upsetting her and that I should stay away. Well, by God, that's what I did. I suppose Bonna didn't want me there because she couldn't see her boyfriend Herb when I was there. It turns out something else was going on, too, only I didn't find that out until later.

So I went up to Menninger's. Then when I came back I found out she was pregnant. Turns out that they had found out about it in the hospital. I think they didn't want to tell me until it was too late to do anything about it. She had just gotten an "A" for an essay against teenage pregnancy, then went out and did it. Bonna was a smart kid. In fact, she was right on the border between bright and genius. So she had to know what she was doing. She always knew what she was doing.

She called the father a puke! I told her, "You don't have to marry this guy. We can work something out." I didn't like him because he was mean. To my mind, a guy who does that to a girl—gets her in trouble—can't really care a lot for her. I thought she should have better than that.

But she wanted the child, so she went ahead and got married. I let her go because I got to thinking about Ray and my trouble with my parents, and I thought, "Maybe they are right for each other. I don't know."

They had a wedding, such as it was. There were no bridesmaids or marching up the aisle. But it was in a church. Bonna wanted that. She had a pretty dress and some flowers. Ernie was smashed half to death. He was too drunk to give her away. I can't remember who did. I was upset myself. She had the baby the day before her 17th birthday. A little girl she named Sandy.

That same summer, Mickey got into some trouble, too. It was a messy summer. Ernie said once, "Well, looks like everything got screwed up." I said, "Well, you set the pattern. So, put up with it."

I could have done away with myself about that time without any trouble at all. I thought about it. After Menninger's I went to a psychologist in Akron. He said I just had to get myself to the place where I could still find a reason to go on living, even if I lost everybody in my family. Well, it just about came to that.

Ernie was the first to go. He was refusing to pay the bill from my Menninger visits. And I was driving his mother up to see his sister in the hospital while he was out chasing some broad.

Finally, I'd had it. I had filed for divorce twice before and never went through with it. It cost me $30 each time, too. But this time, I threw him out. He was up at one of the drying out places he went to. I got all of his stuff together and had it downstairs, waiting for him with a sign that said, "Take this with you." I sent my son to get him and I took off. He went to live in some rooms we had over at the business. I filed for divorce. This time I wasn't going to waste the $30 filing fee.

Bonna went to night school after the baby was born, and I would watch the kid for her. I kind of liked the little girl, Sandy. She'd look at me with those big eyes. Even then Bonna started something with a guy who lived down the street; he was driving her to school. He was married, and she broke that family up, too. It seemed like she just couldn't stay out of trouble.

After she and her husband separated, she came back to live here with the kid. She did not take care of the kid right, I didn't think. She would go out running around and take the kid with her and bring her in at 1:00 or 2:00 in the morning. I told her, "Hey, get yourself in here by midnight with that kid." Well, I'd catch her climbing in the window.

Then she started going around with this girl that I really didn't like. This girl had been married about three times, and I'd heard things about her family. She was wild, and she was a snotty kid. I told Bonna I didn't want that girl over here. But Bonna would bring her here anyway. So one night Bonna had her over, and I called Ernie and told him, "You come up and take this gal out of here and take her home." And so he did. But the next morning when I was going out of the door to go to work, he was there with that girl. He pulled up out front with her in the car with him. I was so furious I just locked the door and I said, "I'm not going to let you in; you'll just wake up Bonna and Sandy." And I went on my way. Left them standing right out there on the sidewalk.

Bonna had started getting real belligerent. I could see it in her eyes. I'm that way too, and I recognized it in her. She had started to tell me that this house was not mine, it was hers, and if I didn't do what she thought I should do, she was going to take the kid away. That kind of thing.

Once when she started that I said, "You just go ahead and take that kid away, Bonna. It's your kid, you do what you want with her." She was trying to blackmail me. So I said, "As a matter of fact, Bonna, you can just leave. You can go down to your dad's." We had a room at the business where she could stay. I said, "When you come back, your stuff will be ready for you." So that was that. She took the little girl and left.

We never did really get together too much after that. Our divorces were in the paper on the same day, in 1965.

In the next four years I didn't set the world on fire or anything but I did finally manage to work for a living. I managed, but it wasn't easy.

Right after the divorce, I worked in a discount store. They let people go, and I was one of them, thank God. I hated that job. Then in '66 I went to work in the library at Kent State. I was dead broke. I also rented out rooms. My next-door neighbor's son, Bob Hagenbaugh, was a good friend, and so when his mother died, he paid for room and board with me—$15 for rent and $15 for groceries every week. It doesn't sound like much, but I only made $195 a month at my job.

With Bob there was nothing romantic. He was a cripple, and crass as all get out. He was also an alcoholic that never did get the program. But before my divorce, he'd helped me an awful lot with Ernie when Ernie was drinking. In fact, that time Ernie smacked me and I left for a few days and left Bonna there, I went to stay with Bob and his mother. So he was like family, coming to room with me. He had a room downstairs, and I had a guy renting upstairs, too. Then, for a while, Mickey was with me.

I had to make a life for myself or I would have gone crazy. I didn't hear too much from Bonna. I heard she went out to Colorado, and it sounded like she was going out to stay, but then she came back. I have this feeling—I can't substantiate it—that she got into trouble with some guy out there. She had a history of that type of thing. Bonna was a beautiful girl.

One day in June 1969, it was the 13th in fact, I was at work at the library, talking to some guy about a record he was looking for. We were looking in the Schwann Record Catalogue, I remember that. Then the phone rang, and I walked over and picked it up. It was Bob Hagenbaugh calling to tell me that he would be up after me. Bonna was dead—shot herself.

I stood there kind of stunned for a few minutes, looking at the phone. I was just blank. I walked back to the Schwann catalogue, and I heard myself talking to the guy, but I just couldn't concentrate on what I was saying. He said, "Is something the matter?" And I said, "Yeah. Maybe you'd better go downstairs and ask the reference department your question." He left, and then I walked over and told the gal I was working with, and we closed up shop. I went and told the gal in the office that I'd got the call and I was clockin' out. And then I waited.

They didn't come for a long time. I couldn't stay in that building, so I went and sat out in the car. One of the gals that I worked with came out and sat with me. I had to get out of that building.

All that time I kept wondering what had happened to Sandy, Bonna's little girl. Well, on the way home on the radio I heard what happened to Sandy. Bonna had shot her, too. I was in shock. I couldn't quite grasp it all. Sandy would have been seven in October. They didn't find them for two days.

I guess I shouldn't have been surprised. I think she was really programmed to do the things she did. In fact, at one time Bonna had mentioned suicide, when she was in her early teens. I got worried and took her over to Ginny's, and we talked. I thought a lot about it. What could somebody that age possibly have to kill themselves over? No reason to talk that way, I didn't think.

It was hot, but I couldn't feel it. We stopped, and Bob got a cold six-pack for me, and we went home and sat on the porch. I just couldn't think of too much. One of the neighbors came up to chat. Later he read it in the paper and told me, "There I was talking to you about nothing, and you had all that on your mind and didn't say a thing."

Then Ernie called me up and chewed me up really good. We had been divorced four years by then, and he was remarried. He said he didn't want me going to Bonna's funeral. I said, "I don't have to go to the funeral. I will make my peace with Bonna whether I'm there or not." He blamed me, although, like I said to him, she did it with his shotgun. He wanted to know why I couldn't have relented toward Bonna, and this, that, and the other. I said I didn't know.

I asked him how she could have done it with his shotgun. I mean, how are you going to hold the thing? He tried to explain how it could be done, but I couldn't see it.

Then my son came in the back door, crying like crazy. He and Bonna were only 18 months apart. They got along good. When I told him his dad didn't want me there at the funeral, he said, "You are going. You have to go." I said, "Don't worry about it, I'm going." And I went to the funeral.

That night we went out to the cemetery, Ernie Jr., Ginny, and I. We sat there in the dark by the graves, looking at the sky. And Ernie Jr. said, "You know, I just have the feeling she's up there laughing at us."

I cried a lot. I had to pray a lot, and I had to block a certain amount of it out of my mind. Sometimes I really felt like I had failed. Then, on the other hand, I didn't feel too badly about my relationship with her because I had tried right before she left home to help her out. The only reason I didn't want her running around with that one girl was because Bonna was going to get a divorce at that time. I thought maybe Herb, her first husband, just for spite, would try and take that baby away, you know? Not that he would want the baby especially, but just to spite Bonna. He was a mean man. So I thought she had to be careful, since I knew she loved that baby. I didn't think she'd want to lose her. But I couldn't reach her, I guess.

I heard she ran around a lot after she moved out. She went to Colorado, but that didn't last long. Then I heard she got married again, shortly before she died. She married some guy a lot older than she was—busted up his family, too. She should have known what she was getting into. She got mad at him one time. He had an apartment over here on the west side, and she had a key to it and went over there. He had a nice, white suit, and she put really hot water in the bathtub and put that white suit in and then her bright red sweater and let it bleed all over it.

She didn't give it much of a chance, I don't think, because they were married in March and she killed herself in June. By then she was alcoholic, and they said she was using diet pills, too. She was only 23 when she killed herself—the same age I was when I married Ernie. Even though we weren't getting along, she was still my kid. I still keep asking myself, why? And why little Sandy? Most of the time, though, I just block it out.

I went through phases of feeling guilty. Then I would think she just did it out of spite. She left a note. She didn't even mention me, which was all right, but that's why I say it was just spite. It said something about telling her dad that he was the best dad a girl could have had. Well, if that's the best, she sure didn't have much, did she?

Ernie never got over it. Bonna died June 11, 1969, and he died two years later to the day, June 11, 1971.

You know, Ernie picked out her name. Once when he was running around with some broad out in Fort Worth, I ordered the Fort Worth paper. And there was a letter to the editor in there from a Bonna Lee Galbraith. Same name. That's a little unusual, don't you think? Why would he pick that name?

After that, I had to find a life for myself or I'd probably have done the same thing Bonna did. I suppose I thought of suicide, but I'm too chicken for that. No way. My life is just beginning to be more fun now.

I had some times when I was real down. Ernie was gone. Bonna and her little girl were gone. I had my job up at Kent State and Bob Hagenbaugh was still renting a room. I'd hear him up at night, so I always knew someone was there.

And I still had Mickey. But even that was kind of shaky. Ernie went right on giving the kids anything they wanted after we were divorced. If Mickey wanted to take the car, he'd let him have the Cadillac. If Mickey needed money, he'd let him have his credit cards. So naturally Ernie was the favorite. Mickey even tells me today, "I always knew I could get what I wanted with Dad, but not with you." He married Barb in 1964, and they had three kids—a daughter in 1967, another in '68, and a son in 1970. I saw them occasionally. But I wasn't much of a grandmother—not rich enough and not exciting enough.

Sue graduating from high school in 1936.

Sandy as she looked at time of her death at age 6.
Her resemblance to Sue—
the mouth, chin, nose, and eyes—
is striking.

Bonna, as she looked at the time
of her death at age 23.

Then I got a bowel tumor in 1970. But I was lucky. They operated on Friday the 13th, just before my birthday in February, and it turned out it wasn't cancerous. But it took me a long time to get over it.

Finally, the doctor let me go back to work a half day at a time. Then he gradually increased it one hour each week. The week I went back full-time was in May. I thought, "Well, I'm back."

Then those kids were shot dead at Kent State. I thought they would never let us out of there that day. It happened around noon, and after that nobody could work or do anything, we were all so upset. But they wouldn't let us go home. I just about passed out, having to wait there like that. So then they sent me home for a week, and I had to start the process all over again, starting out with half a day. I've never been so tired.

Bob Hagenbaugh died in 1973, and I had a rough two years after that. I was by myself. Sometimes I'd think I could hear him at night, moving around in the kitchen or coming in from the front porch. I'd hear him cough, like he did. I'd wait for the sound of the screen door slamming, but it never came.

It's a wonder I wasn't alcoholic. I could have become one. For years I was afraid of it because I knew in my soul I had the makeup for it. All the components were there. My rebellion from my parents protected me in a way, because I made up my mind, "That's not going to be me." For a long time I was afraid to drink. I didn't start drinking until I started to work in 1966, when I was 48.

Everybody always says you can't be an alcoholic if you're only drinking ale, but you sure can. Whatever your taste happens to be and whatever's on hand will do it. It used to be when I first took a bottle of ale, I could sleep pretty well. So, of course, after one, I figured, "Well, I'm just sitting here, I'll have another one." Then I didn't sleep too good. But I liked it and wanted another one.

I remember Betty and Smitty visiting here once in 1974. They came over before noon and opened some beer. I said, "I don't drink anything before noon." And they said, "Hell, it's noon somewhere." I knew it didn't make any difference if you took it at noon or 6 a.m. or 5 p.m. If you need it, it'll nail you. And I needed it. I just made up my mind, "I'm going to give myself a birthday present," and I did. I quit drinking.

For a while I was just trying to make a life for myself. I tried dating, but it didn't work out. It was always fight, fight, fight. I said, "I don't need this stuff." So I started doing things by myself—painting, crocheting, fixing things around the house. I had Ruthie, my friend from work, and I still had Ginny and Ernie, Jr. And Mickey, sometimes.

I started to notice that I was getting more calls from A.A.s, people who knew Dad or had been in the King School group at the start, people who remembered the coffee and donuts we always had after the meeting, or old A.A.s who were passing through town. They liked to come and talk, share the memories, and have a cup of coffee. Heck, I could have used the same old coffee pot I made coffee in when Bill was living with us. I still have it.

I'd always been in touch with my old friends in the program, like Elgie and Johnny R. He came into the program March 1, 1939, so I guess you would say he was an old-timer. But more and more people were calling or visiting from all over the country. Finally, I thought, "I can't afford to entertain all these A.A.s." So I started letting them take me out sometimes. That was real nice.

There were others—people writing articles and books and wanting to know this and that. When Bill died in 1971, the newspapers called me. Lois came down with the New York people to do some tapes on Founders' Day. In fact, I had my own name in the phone book for several years after I was remarried because when people looked me up, they'd look under the old name. Johnny R. says, "Are you really married? You've got your own name in the phone book." I said, "Yeah, I have it in there, Johnny, but it's just for guys like you."

Since I was seeing so many of the old A.A.s, I decided it was time to read the Big Book. I never had read the whole thing, even though I saw a lot of those stories written around our dining room table and typed up some of 'em myself. So, 36 years later, I decided it was time to read the whole thing.

Every once in a while, I would go to Founders' Day. That's the celebration they have in Akron every year around June 10. Every Founders' Day, Lois would call and we would go to lunch—especially after Bill died. In 1975, I went to the Founders' Day Dinner up at Akron U., where Smitty went to school. It was in the gymnasium. At the big meeting, they asked me to stand up and be recognized, so I did. I stood up and everyone in that big gymnasium clapped. It was an experience. It got me back into A.A. a little bit. I started to feel that it meant something to be Dr. Bob's daughter in a way I hadn't felt before.

So I read the Big Book that summer. And I read other books, too, that I found in the attic. They had belonged to Dad, and when I cleaned out the house on Ardmore Avenue, I brought 'em over here. He had quite a collection, you know. He'd read just about everything he could about spirituality, and this was way before Bill came along. He even had a book called *Basic Teachings of Confucius* and books on Christian healing.

You might say I've come back to A.A. after 50 years, but with a difference. Back in '55 when I went to St. Louis for the A.A. Second International, we had that reception where Bill wanted everyone to stand up and say something. When it came my turn, I just passed; I couldn't speak up. Well, it's different now. I'm not little Susie anymore who wouldn't say anything in school even when I knew the answer. This time, I've got something to say.

9

THE LEGACY OF THE MAN

I have a news clipping here about that TV special, *My Name Is Bill W.*, where he is described as the "A.A. Founder." My father is described as "Bill Wilson's doctor." Well, considering that my father was a proctologist, that's pretty funny.

If it's that bad now, I hate to think of what it's going to be like in a few years, when everybody who was there and knows the truth is gone. I want to restore my father and mother to their place in history before it's too late.

Bill was the writer, so he's been remembered. But I think the only thing Bill brought to Akron that Dad hadn't already thought of was the service part of the program. That was the part that Dad was missing. It took both of them to do it, and that's being forgotten. People always said that if it weren't for Bill, A.A. would still be in Akron, and if it weren't for Dad, Bill would've been selling franchises for it on the street. Dr. Bob was as important as Bill. But Bill lived longer and wrote about himself, so he's the one who's recognized nowadays.

Young people coming into the program don't even know about my dad. Just like they never heard about my mother. And she had family groups going on a long time before Al-Anon was founded. But my mother never made any claims for herself. Bill asked my mother to write the chapter on families for the Big Book, but she didn't want to call attention to herself, so she didn't. He didn't ask Lois, and I hear that really rankled Lois. But now all you hear about is Lois. People forgot about my mother. That *Grapevine* article that Bill was supposed to write after her death never got done. And that is a shame, because it would have shown just how much Mother contributed.

I decided that it was time to speak up. If I don't, who will? So I've been more and more involved in A.A. again, one way or another. We usually get about two calls a day, people just wanting to talk or see us. And I finally got up enough courage to give a little talk, about Dad, Mom, Bill, and the things I remember.

In July 1987 at a treatment center in Pennsylvania, I was scheduled to speak. I still have trouble with agoraphobia, so I went to the doctor and said, "Hey, you've got to help me with this." So he gave me one stage-fright pill. I took it an hour before my talk and I guess it helped. At least I got up on the stage. I don't think I gave a great talk, but the people there were grateful just because Dr. Bob's daughter had talked to them. So that gave me confidence to do another. I'm the one who's grateful. It's given me the chance to come out of myself a little more than I would have.

Meeting people has been the thing that has helped me most. And I mean spiritually, not financially. Morally and spiritually.

It's funny how memories come back to you. Like how Mom always used to say when we dug up the garden, "If it's worth anything, it'll come back up!" One October evening in 1975, for example, I was at home, just thinking about getting dinner. It was nice and fresh outside, like it used to be. The phone rang, and it was Ray Windows, asking me if I wanted a cup of coffee. After 38 years.

His wife had just died and he didn't want to be by himself, so he went to stay with his brother-in-law in Akron. Since he was in Akron, he stopped over to see his dad in the apartment where they'd always lived. His dad was pretty old and was not in good shape. It was kind of hard to be there, so he made the excuse of going out to the drugstore to get cigarettes. That was one of the places we used to go. We could sit there all afternoon. So that started him wondering what had happened to me. Last time he talked to me Bonna was just a baby. So he called me from the drugstore, just like that.

84

Ray came over just like 38 years had never happened. As we were leaving the house, I went out ahead. He held the door open for me and I started down the front steps. Then I turned around and went back and put my arms around him. It just felt right. I always knew he'd be back in my life one fine day.

We drove out of town to a root beer stand. We had a cup of coffee and a hot dog. I had to ask for the hot dog. We stayed out late. He took me by his brother-in-law's, but I wouldn't go in. That's because it was October 10. His wife had died on the third, was buried on the 6th, and this was October 10.

I wasn't really surprised when he called. I'd read in the paper that his wife had died, and I knew I would hear from him. But I didn't think it was going to be that soon.

He made me lose a whole night's sleep and a lot of 'em since. Ray called his sister-in-law and told 'em he'd be late. He got home at 2 or 3 a.m. The next day Ray had to go to West Virginia for a few days. We made a date for when he came back.

We were married on December 19, 1975. He was going to wait until February, but then the cost of marriage licenses was going to go up. Tightwad that he was, he made it in December. I got criticized, but thought, "Phooey, I lost him once, I am not going to lose him again." I didn't care what anybody thought. I'd cared what people thought before and it didn't do me any good.

We got married at his brother-in-law's house. Carl was Ray's wife's brother. Lu was his brother-in-law's wife. She asked me how many would be there, and I said, "Don't worry, it won't be over 175." When he gave me my ring he said, "Now that's the last ring I'm going to give you." He never forgot the one I gave back to his mother.

So after 38 years we were married. I guess that was the way it was supposed to be. Mom and Dad didn't think he was the guy for me. At that time, maybe he wasn't. We probably needed each other more when we did get together than we did back then. We'll never know.

Ray came back and he settled in here with me, cats and all. We've got eight, and they're all outdoor cats. All of them are wild. I guess my favorite is

Sue and Ray on their front porch in 1988.

Bull's-eye, number four. They all come here with their visitors for lunch and supper. They aren't allowed inside except to run through to the food in the kitchen. When that door opens, they're ready.

A few years after we were married, I retired from Kent State. I still have the bottle of wine they gave me at the party. The thing must be vinegar by now. I guess you can tell, we aren't exactly wild partyers. We've been living our quiet life. A.A. has been a part of it, and sometimes, I guess, it's not so quiet.

Ray didn't know much about A.A., so when I got calls from the A.A.s, he wondered about it. At first, he didn't want any part of it. When we got married, I told him, "You'd better get used to it." I said, "They're calling me and we're going to be involved in it." Then when Lois called, he met Lois, and they got along. And now he's as involved as I am. He knows just enough about it to confuse someone to death. He loves to go over to the house on Ardmore Avenue; I can't keep him out of there.

One time we were at a Founders' Day breakfast and some of us were talking about the house on Ardmore Avenue. I said, "Boy, sometime it's going to be too late. That house is going to be torn down or something." Then someone said that something was in the hopper to do something about the house. Well, that was the start. The Founder's Foundation bought the house, paid it off, and that house is now a memorial.

We did a lot of physical work on that house, fixing it up. One day over there, Ray and I worked for 16 hours! Ray and this friend of his helped build the office in the cellar, laid the cement for the cellar, and did most of the woodworking.

We scraped old paint off, and cleaned and painted. It took me about five hours to clean one chandelier. And I cleaned the windows beside the fireplace. I crawled across the mantle from one window to the other just like I did when I was a kid. I told Ray, "I'd never believed back then that I'd be doing the same thing 50 years later!" This was back in 1987. We worked hard. Then we had the big dedication, and Wilbur Mills was there, and Ohio Governor Celeste. It was a real nice time.

Now there's a caretaker. He lives in the attic where Smitty used to be with his screech owl. Ray and I and Betty and Smitty are honorary trustees.

I'm glad the house is saved and that it's open to the public now. It looks good, too. Better than it ever did. I remember the white lace curtains

Sue and Ray in 1988 with the original A.A. coffee pot.

we had on that glass front door. Those things were hard to keep clean. Everything was. Back then the air was full of black soot from the rubber factories, and those curtains would be covered with it. I had to clean 'em every week. Now that the rubber industry's gone, it's easier to keep things nice. Everything looks nicer than it did.

The front yard looks better, too, even though the caretaker has been sick a lot. The spirea bushes, which we had planted to make it look like 1935, are gone. Those things were pretty but they ruined the grass with their roots. The house just doesn't have the flower garden Mom had. She loved her flowers, and I always helped her with them. She kept fresh cut flowers around the house. Not those dried or silk things like they have now. I guess it will never be like it was.

I'm a keeper, you know. I never throw anything away. I've got everything, just about, somewhere in my house. After Dad died and I sold the house on Ardmore Avenue, it all went into the attic: books, photographs, letters, and papers. And I've got other stuff from the house—china, the A.A. coffee pot, all that.

I spend a lot of time in the attic, trying to go through everything and get it sorted. Sometimes I'm up there all day. When the A.A.'s visit, I take 'em through my house and they can see the photographs. I've got 'em all over the walls. There are letters, news clippings, and every kind of document. I've got a regular museum. This way I know where everything is. That's where I'm keeping it, too.

I try to live by the Twelve Steps. And I try to follow the Four Absolutes —we haven't forgotten those here in Akron. That's not a bad way to guide yourself. I don't have quiet times as such, but I do pray a lot. I say my prayers at night, and when I get troubled, I try and keep my mouth shut if I'm mad.

I've had to do a lot of praying, too. Ray had four major operations in nine months in 1987. In February, they went in and worked on the carotid artery, then in May they carved him up again with a quadruple bypass. He wasn't even over that when they went back in and took out a wedge of his lower right lung. That was October 9. On October 14, they opened him up again and took out the rest of the lower lung. It was cancerous. Then he was in the hospital again for back trouble—arthritis, gout, you name it. He's never very well.

Photo of Ray and his brother.

ROY WINDOWS **RAYMOND WINDOWS**

Separated

After more than two years of overseas war duty together with the 37th division, the Windows brothers, Raymond and Roy, are going to be separated for the first time. Their parents, Mr. and Mrs. Frank Windows, 806 W. Market st., received a letter last week saying Roy, 32, is up for furlough and expects to get home; but Raymond, 26, will stay out in the Pacific area.

The brothers, both privates first class, have really seen that Pacific area—New Zealand, New Guinea, the Fiji islands, Guadalcanal. Name the major Pacific land engagements and they've been in them—together—as members of an anti-tank crew. They volunteered together Feb. 5, 1941.

Copy of article on Ray and his brother going to war.

I just try to live from day to day. We've had this time together and I try to be grateful just for that. It's a miracle. He was in the Pacific for five years during the war, going from island to island. He was at the Philippines, New Georgia, Guadalcanal, all the bad ones. He got three Bronze Stars. He saw the bodies pile up on the beaches. He was on one of those beaches when he read in an old Akron newspaper that Suzanne Smith Galbraith had a son in April 1944. He said he just about gave up then. But he made it back, and I'm glad we've had the time we've had.

I've often wondered how I lived so long with everything that's happened. Some A.A. from California said maybe I was meant to be adopted by Dr. Bob so I could come to A.A. now to set the record straight. I'm needed. Maybe this was the way it was meant to be for me. I'm a slow learner, and I needed the time to catch on.

I look back and I don't understand why things had to happen the way they did. I just try and accept it. I think Dad would've come around to accepting Ray. I think Dad was my buddy, and he would've let up. But Mom couldn't. I guess they were just trying to protect me.

Then with Ernie, well, it wasn't all bad. We had some good times. That's what keeps you hanging on, you know. You think the good times are always going to come back. I try not to be resentful. I knew what he was like when I married him. I made my own bed.

And with the kids, I said to Mickey once, "I don't think I was a very good mother. I was a lousy mother, and now I'm a lousy grandmother, and I know it." And Mickey says, "Well, you always gave us lots of love." I said, "Oh, yeah, and what good did it do?" And he says, "Oh, I don't know. I think it did some good."

Maybe it did. Maybe it didn't. It seemed like no matter what I did, it was all going to come out the same. I could only do what I knew, and I just passed it on. Somebody has to break the cycle. Bonna broke the cycle. She sure did. June 10, the birth of A.A., will never be the same, because June 11 comes right after.

I try not to think of Bonna and her little girl. I try not to have my resentments. I try to let go. It isn't easy. I think I know what it was like for Dad because I'm like him, only I think he worked the program harder.

Photo of Sue's son, Mickey, and his children.

93

When I read Dad's story in the Big Book, there's a place in there where he says, "My home life is ideal." That was in 1938, and I can tell you, things weren't ideal. Not for me, anyway. I had to think about that. But you know, he could say that because he was recovering. He was working the program. So for him, I guess things were pretty good. But that didn't make it good for me. Not by a long shot. I had to do that myself. I'm still trying, too.

I used to think A.A. didn't work for me, but it was me that was not working the program. The Twelve Steps don't fail, people do. I keep trying. A.A. is a great gift. Dad knew that, I think. It may take fifty years, but it will be there when you are ready for it.

EPILOGUE

Ray Windows died the evening of August 3, 1989. Sue had been at the hospital all day, and then went home to rest. She was on the phone when the operator broke in on the call. She raced to the hospital, but was too late. She didn't go into the room. She wanted to remember him as she last saw him— a big smile, gallantly waving good-bye from the bed. Ray lived up to his three Bronze Stars all the way to the end.

SMITTY'S STORY

PREFACE TO SMITTY'S STORY

Robert Ripley Smith was born on June 5, 1918, and nicknamed "Smitty."
He was a bright, active boy and missed the steady companionship he needed
from his alcoholic and unavailable father. His most cherished moments were
the long trips he took with his father every year. He acquired his father's
fondness for automobiles, and bought his first car in 1934 at age 16.
His teenage years were characterized by drinking, fast driving, and a need
for "action."

He graduated from high school in January, 1936. He was secretly
married in the same year and a daughter he never saw was born. A divorce
was obtained in 1939, after a discreet interval. He began college at Akron
University in 1936, entered R.O.T.C., and graduated with an accounting
degree five years later. The Army called him in January 1941, right after graduation. He went in as a 2nd Lieutenant to a Quartermaster Corps in Fort
Benning, Georgia. Just when his year was up and he was ready to leave the
Army, the Japanese attacked Pearl Harbor and his separation was delayed
indefinitely. He tested and qualified for the Air Force and went into training,
graduating from Kelly Field in 1942. He joined a B-24, four-engine Liberator
unit in North Africa, covering shipping convoys in the Atlantic.

He arrived back in the United States on Thanksgiving, 1943, and spent Christmas in Akron. He went to his assignment, Clovis Air Force Base in New Mexico, where early in 1944 he met Betty Andersen. They were married in October of that year.

Smitty left the military after his marriage and relocated to Cleveland where he worked and spent a year in close contact with his parents. During this time he also saw Sue and Ernie on occasion. Then in 1946 he moved to Hobbs, New Mexico, where he and a partner bought a business. After the business failed, the family remained in Hobbs and Smitty took a job as a roughneck on a drilling rig. He then worked with a specialty company, learning how to work wells that were still under pressure. The company discovered he was a pilot and asked him to become company pilot, leading to several years of ferrying the company president around on various business and pleasure trips. Meanwhile, Betty was at home in Irving, Texas, outside of Dallas, raising their three children, two daughters and one son. Dr. Bob and Anne visited them there in 1949. Anne died shortly after her return to Akron as a result of pneumonia that developed during the trip.

In 1950, Smitty and Betty attended the first A.A. International, and then took their last long trip with Dr. Bob, a leisurely drive to his hometown of St. Johnsbury, Vermont. Dr. Bob died shortly after, in November of that year.

Smitty quit his flying job and started his own company, working wells under pressure and manufacturing the tools to do it. After accumulating enough capital, he sold out and bought a shallow oil field north of Nocona, Texas. He moved to Nocona in October 1955 and until recently worked his own wells as an independent producer. Both Smitty and Betty have been very active in the community, and Bob is now mayor of Nocona.

10

BOB SMITH AND SMITTY

For most of my life A.A. didn't have any personal meaning. I never told anybody my father was instrumental in starting A.A. Never. Occasionally, somebody would find out about it and ask me and my wife Betty to come to a meeting. We'd do that. It was a good time, and we'd see people we knew who were sober, working the program, and we'd say, "Boy, isn't that good for them. They really needed that." And all the time she and I are partying, drinking, and dancing. And finally we're hiding the booze from each other and having hangovers together, and I'm doing some bizarre things. We were not very interested in A.A. because we wanted to do some drinking and partying.

We knew about alcoholism, but we didn't really know alcoholism. Imagine two people who had the education we had on alcoholism, with both of our parents in a recovery program and both of them successful, and not recognize it in our own home—that was us. Because, you see, we were different. We were absolutely different. It would never happen to us. We knew too much about it. It's hard to explain to people, but that's the way we were. We hung in there with the denial. That old denial I learned as a child was still functioning. That was normal for me.

I guess I'll have to start my story when Sue was adopted because I don't really remember anything prior to that. We were both five at the time. Sue was three months older than I. She was adopted because mother had a miscarriage and couldn't have any more children. So they adopted Sue as a playmate for me. What a playmate she was! She and I fought like tigers. She could beat me up. We didn't hit it off too great.

Prior to that, I played a lot with the little girl next door. Sue took a swing at her after the little kid had had an appendicitis operation, and she got into trouble over that.

Incidentally, I still correspond with that lady next door. When we were kids, I never could figure out why she never invited us into her house. I thought maybe it was because we were second-class citizens because of my father's drinking. I found out later, through talking to her, that her mother was doing a lot of drinking with the lady that lived on the other side of her. Her father moved them away to separate those two. She was probably an alcoholic—something that I never knew or even suspected at the time.

Susie and I started kindergarten together. Due to the slight difference in our age, they held me back and allowed her to go ahead and start grade school. Later, I doubled out of the eighth grade right into high school and caught up with her. I was able to get out of grade school with something like a 98 average, except in deportment, which always seemed to bring my grades down. I got D's in deportment all the time, usually because I was bored. I learned quickly, and then I'd spend the rest of the time horsing around. Consequently, I spent a lot of time in the principal's office.

We were fairly prosperous at the time. Apparently my father's drinking had not progressed to the point where it affected his income. We lived in a modest frame house that they bought on Ardmore Avenue, which was where they started A.A.

It was a pretty happy time. My mother was a very dignified lady. She was the type of lady that led a protected life. She was interested in the proper etiquette, and she was a little bit romantic. She liked to have candlelight dinners if she could, but my father said, "I want to see what I'm eating." So they made an agreement: Dad would let her turn out the center light fixture which was right over the dining room table provided that he was allowed to

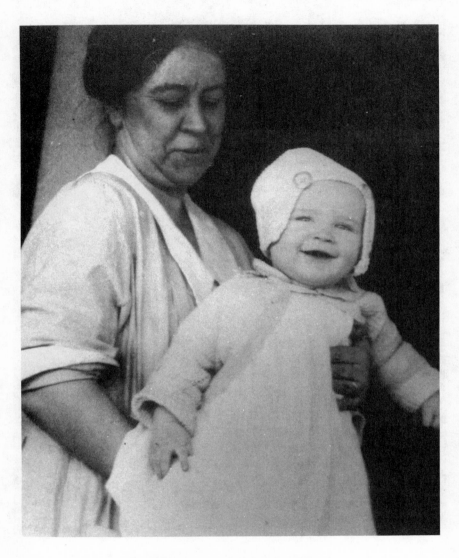

Anne Smith with baby Smitty in 1918.

Dr. Bob and Smitty, on the left,
with next-door neighbor and child.

have the four little corner lights on. Of course, what he did was put four 100-watt bulbs in the corner lights. So she never really got the candlelight dinner.

It wasn't until 1929, when Dr. Bob went back to school, that the poverty really hit. He had been a general practitioner. Then he went back and studied under the Mayo brothers in Rochester, Minnesota, and became a surgeon proctologist. He arrived back in Akron in 1929 at the start of the great "crash" in this new profession which relied entirely on referrals from other doctors. And he had a bad alcohol problem. You can imagine how much business he got.

It wasn't too long after that we became desperately broke. He had bought a new car in 1929 because his old Hudson was stolen. When the authorities found it, he gave the new car to my mother. But we couldn't drive it very much because we didn't have the money. Finally he just stored it because we couldn't even afford the license plates.

My mother took good care of us. She wasn't one of those that played on the floor with us or the huggy-kissy type, but she was warm and sweet, and dignified. She was 38 when I was born; my father was 40.

My mother was very straitlaced. I don't mean she was unkind, but she had had a very straight upbringing. Her family was in management at the Santa Fe Railroad. She grew up in a nice home and became a teacher. She was a graduate of Wellesley, and had gone there on a scholarship. She had been pretty sheltered. Teachers, generally, were called on to lead an exemplary life. That she did, so she was pretty easily shocked.

My father was more the outgoing type, a man who could handle himself among other people well, but he was also very dignified. He never failed to correct our grammar. In a nice way, at the dinner table, we used to see if we could run a few by him. He'd correct us and go right on.

We used to have baseball games out in the street, and Dad would play with us occasionally. What I didn't realize until later on was that the reason he didn't play as much as the other fathers was that he had been drinking. He seemed to have his own regimen. I didn't realize that he was doing things that would allow him to drink more. It wasn't until I was a teenager that I noticed that he never scheduled any operations before eleven o'clock. He arranged things like that to allow himself to recover from his drinking the night before.

Anne, age 3, in one of the elaborate studio portrait settings
favored by well-off parents at the time.
It is indicative of her sheltered, careful upbringing.

Anne's family home in Oak Park, near Chicago. "A nice home," Smitty says.

When I was real little, I never detected any strain between my parents. They never had an open argument—never. Later on, as the alcoholism progressed during our teenage years, we saw that my mother was unhappy. But when we were real little, I suppose our daily lives were typical for the times.

On a typical day, Mother and Father liked to sleep late. So Susie and I would get up in the morning, and I'd go down to the cellar where we had a coal furnace. The fire had been banked the night before, if it was wintertime. I'd fire that furnace up and get it going. I'd dress in a cold bathroom, and then I'd have a bowl of cereal for breakfast. Sometimes by then my father would be up, and we'd catch a ride to school.

We had discipline when we needed it. Mother would use a switch that she cut herself. And she was so wild you never knew if you were going to get hit on the top of the head or the bottom of the feet. She wasn't very scientific about it. We'd finally holler just to get her to quit.

With Dad it was different. It was a real ceremony. Somebody had given us a cat-bat set with a paddle that looked a lot like a ping-pong paddle, which he kept up above the medicine cabinet in the bathroom. When he came home and we had done something wrong, mother would always report it. If we were too bad, then he'd take us upstairs to the bathroom, bend us over, and use that paddle on us.

One time, the little girl next door and I took bars of soap and wrote all over the neighbors' creosote shingles on the side of their house. It was a terrible mess. I don't know why we did that; usually we weren't destructive. I think it cost something like $200 to get the stuff off. Well, Dad was pretty upset about that. I didn't blame him, because $200 was an awful lot of money. I got a good paddling for that.

My mother didn't drive at the time. Dad tried to teach her, but she ran into a woodpile and wrecked his car so he gave up. Later on, when his car was stolen, we got this extra car and he managed to teach her to drive. But she was a terrible driver, just awful. She never did catch on to machinery. All cars had standard shifts in those days. And we had an old car that was very difficult to drive. When Mother finally got to where she could drive, when I was about nine, she began taking us around to some social functions.

Sue, Smitty, and neighbor boy in front.
Photo taken in early elementary school years.

Mother and Father liked to have company over. They had a certain circle of friends. It was a pretty high class deal. They even played duplicate auction bridge. They were both marvelous bridge players. And they didn't run us off when they entertained; we were part of the family.

While my parents often entertained friends, I never saw my mother's family when I was little. I can't even recall her speaking about her mother and father, but I'm sure she must have. Both grandparents had died, so I have no recollection of either grandparent on my mother's side. And my mother had a split with two of her brothers. It started when she and one of her brothers disagreed with the other two about the care of her mother. They never spoke to each other again. It was never healed. They were all very successful men; all of her brothers are in the Who's Who. One of the older ones was an investment banker, a founding partner of Harriman and Ripley, which became Drexel-Lambert, the big junk bond firm in New York. After my father sobered up, he made an effort when he was in New York to call on one or both of the brothers, but he said he just wasn't welcomed. As he put it, they acted like he was going to try to borrow some money from them. They did send a beautiful funeral array at my mother's death, but that was all. My great uncle, Charles T. Ripley, was the president of Santa Fe; later on, the uncle that had sided with my mother became the chief engineer for Santa Fe.

When I was a child, I had kind of a hero worship of my Dad. I was in awe of him. He was a pretty imposing figure. He was so sharp mentally that you knew you weren't going to pull anything over on him. I wished that he could have been more of a buddy to me, but I realize now that he couldn't because of the age difference. And one of the big disappointments in my early life was that my father didn't come to see me graduate from grade school.

Dr. Bob was the type of guy that anyone could talk to and anyone could get along with. He used the slang of the day—not four-letter words, but the modern slang that young people used. He had a prodigious vocabulary, and he was an extremely intelligent guy. He had studied Latin and Greek for many years. He used to speak German when he bought his surgical stuff from the Krupp salesman.

Women felt very comfortable around him, too, because his love for my mother always showed. He had a deep abiding love for that woman, and it was evident. He was always courteous, always a gentleman. He never failed to stand up when a lady entered the room.

He also had a great sense of humor. The elevator operators and the nurses kept him up on all the latest dirty jokes. He used to come home and share them with me. He loved jokes, especially puns. We told each other some of the most horrible puns that we knew. He'd laugh 'til the tears ran down his cheeks and he'd have to take his glasses off.

One special thing I remember that he did with me, even in his drinking days, was to take long hikes on Sundays. Sometimes Susie would go with us, but it was always my dad and I, our dog, and one of the neighbor men.

Both my dad and my mom were very spiritual people. Dad read the Bible from cover to cover several times. Mother loved culture. Her favorite thing was listening to the operas on radio every Saturday afternoon. She sat by that radio, and nobody was to bother her while the opera was on. I thought they were pretty silly. I never got to be an opera buff myself, although I tried. There was a time when I was cultured so I made an attempt, but her passion never really rubbed off on me.

I deeply loved my mother. And I somehow thought that although she was trying hard to control my father's drinking that she just wasn't up to the job. Of course, I realize now that nobody is.

My parents and I didn't have a terribly close relationship. They had a certain way to do things. So when the Depression really got going good, when the poverty really set in on us, they began to get some pretty wild reactions from Susie and me.

A youthful Anne and one of her brothers
in happier times before her estrangement
from all but one brother.

11
POVERTY IN THE SOUL

The Great Depression started coming on when I was 12, around 1930. With Dad's new specialty, he had to rely on other doctors for referrals, and, of course, they knew he was drinking. So he didn't have much business. He kept a few of his old patients who wouldn't turn him loose, and they managed to pay a little bit of the bills, but not much. That's when it started to hit me, when it started getting bad. That's when the poverty set in. That's also when I started to be aware of Dad's drinking.

Mother got very tearful at that time. She'd cry when she'd confront him. And he would promise that he wouldn't take another drink in front of us, and mean it, I'm sure. Mother was a teetotaler; she never drank anything. It was beyond her. One time she had tried to get us to put on a little act for him. She said to tell him she got drunk. She took a little drink of whiskey, and pretended to be drunk, putting on the worst act of a drunk I ever saw. It was so bad it was embarrassing. It embarrassed him, and it embarrassed us. I don't know what it did to her.

I never heard them have angry words. Never. They must have had arguments, but not in front of us. When they had the discussions about Dad's drinking—the begging and the promises—we heard some of that. I asked her one time, "Mom, you had so much trouble with him, why didn't

113

you leave?" And she said, "I didn't have any place to go; my parents were dead."

My method of handling Dad's drinking—and this was pretty standard in our family for a long time—is that I didn't mention it. I never discussed it with any of my friends. I acted like it was non-existent. When Mother lied to the patients on the telephone by saying, "The doctor is out of town" and that sort of thing, it never bothered me.

I don't remember feeling any anger or resentment about the drinking, but I resented the poverty. I didn't like that a bit. The poverty we experienced wasn't an instant deal, it was kind of phased in as the Depression deepened and worsened. There were times when Mother had maybe two dollars a day to buy groceries for the whole family and whoever else dropped in. We often had just bread and milk for dinner. We finally got down to where there were almost no new clothes. My father tried to keep a decent suit or two, but the rest of us were in pretty bad shape, even though my mother was a very frugal shopper. She bought things to last, like the shirt she bought for my eighth grade graduation that was so big I could still wear it when I graduated from high school!

We almost lost the house. Before the Depression, Dad told me, he had the money to pay off the last $1,000. But the old mortgages used to be written so that even if you paid them off, you still had to pay all the interest. So he didn't pay it off. Well, the time came when he couldn't even make the mortgage payments. We would have been thrown out in the street if hadn't been for the mortgage moratorium declared by President Roosevelt in 1933 that allowed people to stay in their homes even though they couldn't make the payments. Akron was a one-industry town—rubber—and times were bad.

I could see that we were poorer than the kids I traveled with, or wanted to travel with. They all had more than I had. Of course I resented that, and material things became very, very important to me. This is clearly a character defect of mine.

I didn't think of anybody but myself. Everything I did was strictly for me, and my father told me that I was the most selfish person he had ever met in his life. I guess one reason I must have been that way was to try and build myself up because we were so broke.

Smitty at age 16 with his first car (1934).

I finally got a paper route. It covered a couple of city streets and a few estates like Harvey Firestone, Jr.'s and the treasurer of Firestone's—very wealthy people. It took me a long time to complete that route because it was about seven miles. Most of it was through these gorgeous estates. Afterwards I would go back to our little house, but those gorgeous estates stayed in my mind. I thought everything I needed was behind those gates.

As soon as I could, at age 16, I bought a car. That's when I really set sail. I stayed out in that old car as long as I could. It was a frantic type of fun. I had to have action.

I bought an old Chevy with brand new tires on it, then wore them out in 4,000 miles. That's how hard I drove that thing. I hardly had any money. You know, 25 cents for gasoline and 25 cents for entertainment, and that was it. The paper route only paid a dollar and five cents a day. But I had a car and I was pretty cool. Of course I had to do all the work on it myself.

Before I had a car of my own, I was just dying to be able to drive. My mother's car was parked in one of the neighbor's garages, and I would steal it. When they took the key away, I had a key made. Then they took the rotor out of the distributor, so I got another rotor. Finally they took the battery out, so I came up with a spare battery. It took me a little longer to get going because I had to put the battery in, put the rotor in the distributor, and then use my key to steal her car. Sometimes I had to be sure to wash it when I brought it home so it looked as clean as it was when I took it out. You can tell from that I wasn't a constant source of joy to those people.

It's difficult to relate my emotional state at that time. I didn't feel angry, but I had a sense of fighting a second-rate feeling. I don't know if that accurately describes it or not. I wasn't angry at my parents. I've never felt angry at them. I was too busy entertaining myself to be angry with them. And I didn't feel hurt. It seems that I got away with everything I could. I just laid low and did things my way. I didn't stand up to them and slug it out like Susie. I didn't have her resentment then, and I still don't.

By that time Mother started losing her social circle and stopped entertaining. That becomes a necessity in a home with active alcoholism because you never know what the conditions are going to be. She had a lot of family pride. It was very important to her to hide the alcoholism from the general public, and that included her friends. So her social life just stopped.

I had a general fear that people knew about Dad's drinking, because it was becoming pretty apparent. He wasn't a telephoning drunk or a running drunk or anything like that. He was a pretty quiet drunk. He didn't drive while he was drinking. The boys from the Central Garage were trained to bring him home. Our garage was under our house. They would drive him in there and close the garage doors. They were young guys, and they were sympathetic. They liked him. Everybody liked old Doc. All we had to do was get him upstairs and get him to bed and he'd stay there. It really wasn't a problem.

Often he would escape. He would go out and check into a hotel under an assumed name because he didn't want my mother to scold him. She'd have to try to find him, which was very difficult for her, especially when she didn't drive. After she got her own car, she was mobile, and it was a little easier to find him.

Many times we would all haul him up the stairs from the garage. Some pulling. Some pushing. But once we got him up the stairs, got his clothes off, and laid him in the bed, he was out like a light.

When you see someone like that, I think you begin to feel pity and disgust. And bewilderment. A sense of loss. Because this person that you love is totally out of it.

When he was himself, he was a neat guy to be around. He used to take me downtown and buy me sodas. They had the cigar store down in the basement at the bottom of the Second National Bank Building, his office building, and I'd get a soda and he'd get a Bromo Seltzer to get through the morning.

If my friends knew about Dad it wasn't because I gave it away, because I never discussed it. I went through great lengths to hide it. That's how I think I managed to avoid the worst effects of it. I just never invited my friends into the house if I knew my father was going to be home because I never knew what shape he was going to be in. So all you had to do to get me was to honk the horn and I'd run outside. My method of coping was to escape. And it worked, I think, although I always carried with me the feeling that something was wrong, that we just weren't quite up to snuff as far as other people were concerned.

I remember once when my mother decided to take the wallpaper off. She enlisted my dad's aid, even though he had absolutely no mechanical ability whatsoever. He ran the garden hose through the bay windows and started squirting the walls. My mother almost fainted. So she shut him down, and the job of scraping the wallpaper fell to Susie and me.

Well, we'd scrape a while, then we'd fight a while. We took after each other with the furniture. It wasn't just fists. We took chairs and everything else. Then we'd have to stop the fight and straighten the place up before the folks got home. We banged up some of Mom's prized possessions and then tried to glue them back together.

Sue and I didn't do any of our real fighting around our parents, just the kind you'd find in a normal brother-and-sister relationship. We weren't very close. We had entirely different friends, and we went our separate ways. She was very resentful, a belligerent kid. We were just each involved in our own survival.

When you're raised in our kind of a home, the alcoholic is busy drinking and the spouse is busy trying to keep him from it. Both are full-time occupations. They don't have much time for you, so you just go on your merry way and survive any way you can. There isn't much supervision because the parents don't have time. They were very busy people.

I did have some fun and some good times with my dad, though. He went back to St. Johnsbury, Vermont, for a visit every year. He loved to go back, and I would go with him. Mother was smart enough not to ride with him. I don't think she particularly liked Grandmother Smith, who was kind of a stern person. I thought she was selfish. When we were there Dad drank during the whole trip.

I remember one year he drove an old Cadillac coupe. It was a terrible old car, a real clunker, with bad gas mileage and vapor lock. He had to add kerosene to the gasoline for the vapor lock. We called it the Ark and we called him Noah. We thought that perhaps if he took the car down into the poorer section of Akron and left the motor running, maybe somebody would steal it. He stuck with the old thing 'til the day he went out to get in it and stepped through the running board. Then he bought himself a second-hand Pierce Arrow, which we called the Fierce Error. At any rate, when we made this trip to Vermont, he still had that old Cadillac. Susie and I both went with him, and he drank all the way.

He got into the beer on the way up, so I got to do the driving. Of course, I wasn't old enough to drive but I loved it, even though I had to look through the steering wheel. He sat over in the right seat, throwing the beer cans out the window. A state trooper in New York stopped us. I guess the car looked like a runaway with just my head sticking up. He made my father get back under the steering wheel and drive, and he didn't say anything about Dad's drinking. When he got to the Vermont-New York border, he really loaded up with beer because he thought Vermont was dry, even though it had gone wet in the meantime. After he sobered up, we went down to visit some of Mother's relatives who had some beach property in Duxbury, Massachusetts. They were well-to-do people; they had their own tennis court. If I remember right, he played six sets of tennis with Susie and me. Now this is a guy in his middle 50's, and he wore us both completely out.

Another year, I had an old Ford Model "A" roadster that I bought with a friend of mine named Tom Grant. Dad, Tom, and I went back to Vermont in it. We only paid $12.50 for it, and it had no top. I had said, "Dad, this car doesn't have a top. What are we going to do when it rains?" And he said, "We're going to get wet." He was just as much fun as any kid and was not the least bit self-conscious. Here was a medical doctor, riding in this old Ford with two wild, teenaged kids.

The following year we went and toured the West in another old, open car, a Model "A" touring car. The car didn't have any windows, and we had to throw all the food out in Yellowstone Park or the bears would have torn us to pieces. We went through Yellowstone Park and Wyoming and the Dakotas and into Chicago to see Mother's brother.

By the time we showed up to see the relatives in Chicago, we were quite a sight. We were badly sunburned. Our lips were all cracked. Dad had on an old long-sleeved shirt with his short-sleeved shirt under it. But that didn't bother him because he always had dignity, regardless of how he happened to be dressed.

We showed up in Chicago with no muffler. We had sawed the muffler off so the old car would keep cool. Our uncle lived out in Wilmette, which is still a pretty high-class part of Chicago. It's full of big, gorgeous homes. My uncle was quite welcoming, even though we showed up in this old car with no muffler. The uncle was a lovely guy and had married a lovely lady. They had three nice kids. We kept in touch for a while, but we don't anymore.

As for me, I was totally involved in myself. I wasn't really close to anybody. I was a user. I couldn't be a very good friend because the friends I had were people who I thought could be of some use to me. I wasn't a very desirable person at that time.

I would siphon two gallons out of Dad's old car every day to make it to school and back. Well, he wised up to that and got one of those anti-theft things and put it in his gas tank. I soon found out that by taking a big screwdriver and sticking it in there and prying the spring apart, I could take a small siphon hose and put it down in his tank and get the other end in my two-gallon can. That gave me just the time I needed to stoke the furnace and go up and eat my breakfast. When I came down, I had two gallons of gas. Then I'd go off to school.

One day I failed to put the gas cap back. When he backed out of the garage, it fell off the trunk and he heard it rattle, and then he knew what I'd been doing. But he didn't get mad about it. He just laughed and said, "Why that little fellow."

I think that kind of behavior was part of the protective mechanism I developed as a result of being in an alcoholic home. You have a real shroud around you, and you just operate like you're in a tunnel. You don't care or think about other people. You never let people know what you're really thinking or feeling. I was pretty hard to reach. As far as true feelings went, I had 'em pretty well hidden. I just didn't feel 'em.

I started drinking when I was about 16. I always had to be home by 1 a.m., and I had to pass Mother's inspection. I called it the sniffing committee. So I would try all kinds of tricks, like eating maple leaves, and apparently it worked because she never said anything about it. She was so set against booze, you know. She made me promise never to take a drop. I broke that promise many times.

But I think all the time that my father's drinking was getting worse, Susie and I kind of built a shield around ourselves and operated on our own. We stayed away as much as we could. We were embarrassed. We felt like second-rate citizens.

I was a pretty restless sort of guy. I was always looking for action, anything for excitement. Once the insurance man called Mother about my insurance and said, "I finally figured out who your kid is." This guy lived on a slick, straight brick street. I used to have an old Ford, and whenever it rained, I would take that old Ford out and get it going as fast as I could. Then I'd throw the brakes on and see how many times I could make it spin before it stopped. I didn't know that one of the men who lived on that street was the guy that had me insured!

Most of the time I didn't get caught. Occasionally I did. I had one job where the Chrysler dealer in Akron would pay us high school kids 50 cents each to go up to Cleveland, pick up these brand-new cars, and drive 'em back. Well, we were on our way to Cleveland, speeding as usual, and we got stopped in this little town. The local police stopped us, arrested the driver, and took him to jail.

All of us were wandering around this courthouse. I wandered into the mayor's office and decided I just had to go to the bathroom, so I peed right there in the mayor's spittoon. The local policeman came in right when I was in the act. Of course, he was pretty upset about it.

I was never officially charged. He threw me in the slammer along with this other kid. Then we had to make arrangements to get out. Luckily, it never showed up on my record. What was bad was when I had to explain to my father why I was in there.

I had a Ford V-8 roadster when the cops still had Model A's, and I spent many a happy night tantalizing them because they couldn't catch me. I was deliberately asking for a chase. The Ford had spotlights on it and I used to flush out the lovers. I'd shine the spotlights, just to make them furious. They thought it was the police, and they'd start chasing me. That was fun. I loved the excitement of it. But then I got a young girl pregnant and had to marry her. So that dampened my style. I was 18.

My father was barely sober then. It was a terrible blow to my parents now that I look back on it. I was the great white hope, and I really screwed up.

I went off and married this girl and didn't tell them until a few weeks later. They didn't kick me out of the house, but they were absolutely devastated. And, of course, it was a bad time for me and the girl.

We got a divorce after two years, and she's dead now. I paid child support for eighteen years. When I wasn't able to, my father did. I don't know where my daughter is.

But marriage and fatherhood stopped my social life. It was quite a stigma at that time. You can't imagine what it was like. You can't keep something like that a secret. I went to college with an awful stigma—married. I wasn't living with her. We never lived together. I couldn't date any girls, of course, until I got the divorce. That was an awful scandal, too.

I think that was really the first time I became aware that my actions hurt my parents. They weren't aware of a lot of the stuff I did. I never did tell 'em, either.

But when I had to get married, and I had to tell them, I just wanted to hide. I had a terrible sense of shame and guilt. I felt totally ostracized, even though my folks gathered around me and supported me.

Since I was their only natural child, of course my parents had high expectations. Every parent does. But I didn't take it seriously. My father made me go to college. All I wanted was to get a job at the gas station, and put squirrel tails on the antenna of my Chevy. I didn't want to go to college. I wasn't interested, and I was awfully mixed up. I had other interests. I had a motorcycle and I took trips with a buddy—anything to get out.

I don't know how Dad got me to go to college, but he was a pretty forceful guy. I started out to become a mechanical engineer because my uncle thought that would be a wonderful field. My uncle had once offered to put me through Northwestern University in Illinois, but that offer ended when I screwed up so bad and got married. I went to Akron University, a streetcar school.

I think I got the divorce in 1939. I still had three years of college to go, and I was looked upon as pretty substandard. I compensated for it by just going my wild way. I was on probation for two years but they didn't kick me out thanks to a kind, young dean. I did terrible in school. You ought to see my transcript. The only "A" I ever got was in R.O.T.C. I just didn't care.

12
DESTINY

Mother had been involved in the Oxford Group for years before Bill W. came to town. I think it gave her hope for the first time. Somehow she talked my father into going. Even I went five or six times. I wasn't totally disinterested. A little of it rubbed off on me, but I usually went just to get out of the doghouse for something. I thought the Oxford Groupers were kind of overzealous.

The meetings were held in the basement of T. Henry Williams' home. He had a beautiful home. He and his wife Clarace were such gracious, kindly people. T. Henry looked more like an honest-to-god alcoholic than any human I ever saw—red-faced, with a real port-wine nose with red veins. And I don't think he ever even had a drink.

There were 20 people down there in the basement on folding chairs. At the time, I wasn't aware of what it was going to develop into. I didn't think about it. I was just doing my duty to get out of trouble.

Then one Sunday Henrietta Seiberling called, and I didn't have anything else to do, so I drove over there with Mother and Dad. It was a beautiful day. The sun was shining. Dad said he'd only spend 15 minutes talking with this guy, Bill, whoever he was, so I thought, "That's plenty," and I rode out with them.

My father had a little coupe. It only had room for three people, so Susie stayed home. She had her own plans. They weren't the type of parents to just drive off and leave us. They tried to involve me as much as I let them. They were loving people. It was just that I was the one who wouldn't accept the love. I'd accept just so much, and then the barriers went up. They were up that day, too.

We arrived, and Bill was there. Of course, Henrietta was very gracious and very open. She was the epitome of the cultured southern belle. But Henrietta was also pretty outspoken, and she said, "Here's a man who thinks he can help Dr. Bob." When she introduced Dad to Bill, she did not beat around the bush. Bill was very open. He was an easy guy to meet.

After dinner, they went off in a room by themselves, and I stayed in the house a while. Then I went out and played around outside. It was a huge estate with gorgeous grounds. It got late, I remember. I don't remember anything being said on the drive home, or anything being said about it the next day.

Nobody ever explained anything to us kids. I guess nothing was happening at first. Alcoholics Anonymous was just a gradual build-up from absolutely nothing. That's what it started from—nothing. I think, through the guidance of a loving God, somehow the two of them were able to put together a program.

Originally Henrietta got Bill a room at the Portage Country Club. About two weeks later, he came to live with us. I had to move up into the attic. Since I was out as much as possible, I didn't mind. I just needed a place to sleep.

Then my father went off to his medical convention in Atlantic City. He got the urge, and got terribly drunk. But he didn't come right home. He got the office girl Lillian and her husband Everett to come get him at the station, and they took him up to their house. People just loved to help old Doc and sober him up. They took him in and worked on him. Then they told Mother where he was. By the time they called Mother, it had been five days since he left Atlantic City, and he was still in bad shape. Mother and Bill had to work on him for two or three days more, and then he did an operation on June 10. He took his last drink that day, a beer to steady his hands before the operation. That marks the official birth of A.A.

A portrait of Dr. Bob not usually seen.

I don't remember much else about that day. I had a life of my own, such as it was. But I started seeing things happen. When the other drunks started coming into the house that summer, that was fun.

I remember when Eddie R. came. He was a young, good-looking guy with dark hair. He had a darling long-haired wife, a little-bitty woman, and two little kids, and Mom and Dad moved them right into our house. It was kind of funny. We had these downspouts around the corners of the house. They'd lock Eddie in Susie's bedroom and he would slide down the downspout. They wanted to sober him up, but he kept escaping. Then Dad would get the car and Bill would set out on foot, and they'd chase Eddie down and recapture him. One time Eddie got as far as Cleveland. He called them up, and told them he was going to commit suicide. But he gave them time to come up and witness the event.

Finally it was decided that the only thing they could do for Eddie was to take him back to Ann Arbor and recommit him to the mental institution. It turned out he had an underlying mental problem that came out when they sobered him up. And that was a terrible blow to Bill and Dr. Bob. It felt like failure.

But there is a beautiful ending to Eddie's story. At my father's funeral in 1950, a guy walked up to me and said, "You know me?" I said, "Yeah, I know you. You're Eddie." He said, "That's right." He said, "And I'm a member of the Youngstown group and I've been sober one year." But, early on, Eddie was a big blow.

Then they found Bill D. I knew Bill pretty well because he handled my divorce, for one thing. He was an attorney, a slow-talking southern gentleman. His wife had a job working out at the workhouse where they housed the women prisoners. Bill's practice of law had diminished down to nothing, even though he was a very able politician when he was himself.

These were three very determined people—Bill W., my mother, and my father. They worked on Bill D., and he was a success. And then more came. But you have to remember this thing was not an instant victory. It was a tough, tough row, with lots of heartaches, lots of egos. We were very unpopular. We had taken these drunks into our home because of the Depression, and it was like someone had moved a halfway house next door. You can imagine how popular they were in the neighborhood.

Then we got kicked out of the Presbyterian Church. The minister, J. Carroll Wright, lived on our street, the fourth house down from ours. We had been going to that church because it was convenient. As I remember, it was kind of nice. It catered to the wealthier part of town.

Mr. Wright came down to our house and told Dad that it would be better if we just didn't attend that church anymore, that it was causing a lot of friction among the congregation. What he was trying to tell him was that alcoholics weren't very desirable and they weren't really church material. My mother and father were very hurt.

The upshot of it was that they joined the Episcopalian Church and stayed with it until they both passed away. That was Dr. Tunks' Church. He was the minister who Bill first called, and he delivered the funeral oration for Dad. I used to date his daughter.

A.A. endured a terrible struggle when it started. It was looked down on as a cult of undesirables—untouchables in our society. They were thought to be a bunch of nuts. Getting kicked out of church wasn't the only type of snub they were getting.

In the beginning, I doubt that Bill and Dr. Bob could have raised $50 between them. That's how bad it was. But they had open, spiritual minds. My father was interested in that sort of stuff. He was probably a better student of it than Bill because he had spent a lot more time on it. He had been forced to go to church for so long as a boy that he said many times that he was allergic to "sky pilots"—his nickname for ministers. But he had been searching. His readings had been spiritual as opposed to what you might call religious.

After he sobered up, Dad took Susie and me around to different churches. We went to the Jewish synagogue and to the Catholic church and to all the Protestant denominations, and even heard the Bible as interpreted by Mary Baker Eddy. He used to laugh because once in a while he'd have a patient that was a Christian Scientist, and, of course, they always said that they were the reflection of God. I'd say, "Dad, how come they would come to you, an M.D.?" And he'd say, "Well, I guess they must have a little dust on the reflector."

I think maybe he was trying to teach us that every person has their own concept of God. No two of us have the same conception. Of course, I didn't get it. God had been used to improve my deportment which did need improvement. But I was wild. I wasn't ready for anything like "God as we understand Him."

You've got to realize that both Bill and Doc had real presence. They were both characters. Bill was a casual type of guy. He'd take his shoes off and prop his feet up on the table and smoke cigarettes. They would talk, talk, talk, and drink coffee. Bill was a frustrated musician, and a terrible violin player. He said he had taken off a year of his life to learn the violin. It was not a very productive year, I'll tell you. But it didn't bother Bill.

My father, although the quieter one, had a certain presence, too. So our house was very much full of those two guys and my mother giving them guidance in her quiet way. Not that I was interested in A.A., but I was glad to be around these two vibrant characters.

When Dad sobered up, he was in great shape physically. He never was sick until his final illness. Never. Plus he had a great sense of humor. He had nicknames for everybody. He called me "Smit," and Susie was "T" after a character he heard of someplace called "Hortensia Twitchbottom." And he called Sister Ignatia, "Ig." That was the sort of close relationship they had. I knew her well. She was a delightful person, a frail little lady with a very soft, quiet voice. But she had that certain something that, when she spoke, everyone understood that's the way it was going to be. She never raised her voice. She was very, very fond of Dr. Bob, so they worked together great as a team.

As for the drinking, I didn't feel right away that anything was changing for Dad. As far as I was concerned, my attitude the first day they stopped drinking was "so what?" because you figured they were going to start again. But I gradually saw that the drunks would come in, they'd start to brighten up, and pretty soon you'd have a real person.

I was at a particularly difficult time in my life when all this was happening. Or I thought I was. And when all these drunks started coming through, something happened for me. I felt like I fit in with these people. They all had big problems. They were all misfits in some way. They were all rejected. I fit right in. It wasn't something I understood, I just felt it. Here were people that could accept me.

During this time, I lived partly at home and partly at the frat house. I lived at home when I could because there was always food there. They served lunch at the fraternity house, but that was the only meal. Lunch was

25 cents and the dues were $4 a month. It was always cold because we never could afford to buy enough coal to keep the furnace going. It was a big, old mansion that we rented.

I didn't resent sleeping in the attic at home. The attic in that old home was finished off. It had plaster walls. It was originally for a maid. Being such a modest home, I never understood why it had provisions for a maid. But that was kind of the thing at the time.

I liked being at home because there was a lot of action. I didn't do too well at school because I took off every chance I got. I don't know how old Doc kept me in school, but he did. I kept trying and he kept paying for it. It wasn't very expensive, although it was a lot for those days. Tuition was $34.

I'd stay at the fraternity so I could escape any time I wanted. When I was there, nobody knew when I came and when I went. When I first started at Akron, no fraternity was even interested in me, which was another rejection. I had a car and I also had a motorcycle, so I could get around. But I didn't even pledge a fraternity until I was either a sophomore or junior.

I didn't have any idea what I was doing in college. I started out to be a chemical engineer even though I had never taken chemistry in high school. I flunked that, then just kind of flubbed around a while. I decided that maybe since math came easy to me, I could major in accounting. So that's what I did. It was a tough major. A lot of guys started out in accounting, but not many graduated.

I finally decided that the only way I was going to get out of college was to start studying a little bit, because apparently they weren't going to kick me out. In spite of my best efforts, they kept me. So I actually started trying to be a better student.

Fortunately I made it, either by luck or fate. And accounting has been damned useful. There have been times in my life when I had to do some extra work. You know, I had two girls in college at the same time and I had to go to work for other people. I couldn't make it with my little oil business, so I fell back on my accounting.

Once the district judge called me and said, "The county auditor just had a heart attack. Will you come down to work for us?" I said, "Sure." So, I went down and I was the county auditor. And I worked as the county treasurer because the treasurer was sick. Before that, when the girls were in college, I assessed the value of all the oil properties and utility properties in

Smitty, at age 17, a picture of adolescent angst.
"I always had that feeling that I carried with me—
that we just weren't quite up to snuff as far as
other people were concerned. I was pretty hard to reach."

the county. I always prided myself on being an independent oil producer, which I liked because I was my own man. I did it my way. I looked after the wells when I wanted to, and I wasn't responsible to anybody but myself. It was the perfect job. So when I needed it, I could use the accounting I learned in college.

It was entirely by accident that I acquired that skill. When I was in college, I didn't think ahead. Not a bit. I've always had short vision.

I hate to tell you this, but I was ever so shallow. I wanted money—not for money's sake—but so I could buy things. Whatever was lacking, I would make up for it with things. The money itself was of absolutely no interest to me. I wanted purchasing power, and I loved to chase girls. That was it. Mom and Doc and Bill were out bringing the drunks into the Oxford Group and evolving a program. I was floundering around and just making it through college, I am convinced, through divine intervention and my father's iron will.

Eventually the Oxford Group practices of open confession and getting guidance, plus the resentment the nonalcoholics had for all the alkies who were starting to come in, made it imperative that they split off. Of course, Dr. Bob and my mother didn't want to do it. It was a pretty wrenching experience for them. Dr. Bob was a sensitive guy, a very loving person, and it really tore him up. Things like that, that involved people that he trusted deeply, tore him apart.

Clarence S. and Dorothy, his wife, led the revolt from the Oxford Group. I'm a fan of Dorothy's. And Clarence did a lot of good in his lifetime. Clarence was also a big fan of Dr. Bob's, but he didn't like Bill. Clarence wrote many nasty letters to Bill. But he loved Dr. Bob. I saw Clarence again at a regional conference long after A.A. was established as a worldwide organization. I remembered him right off the bat. They wanted us to come to Florida where he was giving spiritual retreats. We never did make it.

After the alcoholics broke away from the Oxford Group, they held meetings in our home. But there were 72 people at our house one time and that was too many. That's why they started the King School group, which is still in existence, although in a bigger place.

My mother at this time seemed to have infinite patience. You've got to realize that some of the things that she was hearing were absolutely shocking to her because she had been so protected. But somehow she gracefully accepted all that happened. She accepted the snubs and humiliation, the things that went with this new movement. She seemed to be able to keep her eye on the course.

She got the idea, almost immediately, of involving the family in the program. She started having family group meetings as early as 1936. My father and Bill were out making Twelfth-Step calls and Mom was on the phone doing the scheduling and talking to the wives and the sweethearts. There were times when she was able to do more than the guys could. There was one guy—some wealthy banker, Bob E., I think—who relied entirely on my mother for his sobriety. His recovery was a slow process, but she never lost patience.

Bill himself has said that Anne Smith is the Mother of A.A., and I have wondered if maybe they might have quit if it hadn't been for my mother's continuing, unfailing support. Doc and Bill would get so discouraged. There were big egos and big fights over the writing of the Big Book. There was a lot of suspicion. There was even a rumor around Akron that Dr. Bob and Bill had known each other well before they met at Henrietta's, that this was a con job they were putting on people.

Some of the stories for the Big Book were written in our dining room. The guys would come over and sit at the old dining room table with a yellow tablet and a Big Chief pencil. They weren't literary people. This thing wasn't easy. A lot of guys thought they ought to get paid for it. Bill D. was one of them. He thought he ought to get paid for his story, you know. And, if I remember right, his story is not in the first edition of the Book.

At my age, I didn't have the vision to realize that a great movement was being started. My idea of the whole thing was, "Well, maybe . . . " Maybe the book will sell. Maybe the program will take hold. I was kind of skeptical, but Bill and Doc had great hopes.

The book didn't exactly burn up the bookshelves. It wasn't an instant best-seller. But they persevered. These guys had guts. And they had my mother. I really believe she kept them going. But it was also prompted by a sense of survival. When they finally sobered up they realized, "We're talking about survival, folks. We're not talking about some obscure disease of the distant future. We're talking about life and death. Your life and death. My life and death." It was very personal to them, although it didn't mean anything to me. Not at the time, anyway.

13
TIME OUT

In 1939, when the Big Book came out, I just lived from day to day. I didn't have a future. I had no idea what I was doing. I got my divorce. My father, though, began getting back on his feet professionally. Doctors did not get rich in those days, but he began to be able to help me out more financially. I was able to quit my paper route when I was a junior and he saw me through college with an allowance. So things were looking up in that regard. Money was my ticket to the good times. That's what I wanted.

I made it out of college in 1941. It took me five years plus two summer sessions. I went right into the service. What really turned me around and made me a man was going into the service. Not that I planned it that way. I was a reserve officer. I had taken ROTC for four years in college, not inspired by patriotism, but because they paid a little money. It wasn't much, but it was something.

I was called in January of '41. I was thrilled to death to have a job. I was commissioned as a second lieutenant in the Quartermaster Corps and sent to a truck company in Ft. Benning, Georgia. You know, the Army, in its infinite wisdom, sent me to a truck company because I majored in accounting.

I was tickled to go. I was scared to death I wouldn't pass the physical. Susie moved out of the house about a month after I left. I didn't become

Smitty as Air Force officer, 1944.
"I became even wealthier—
a second lieutenant didn't get much,
but, boy, I spent every dime I could make."

estranged from the family though. We stayed close. I know they objected to her marriage to Ernie. They thought it was awful. He was so much older. During my first month in the service Dad wrote me about the *Saturday Evening Post* article, although I didn't realize the significance at the time.

The military didn't changed me, although I became even wealthier. A second lieutenant didn't get much, but, boy, I spent every dime I could make.

It was supposed to be a one-year deal. I had my orders to come back home when Pearl Harbor happened. Of course, those orders were cancelled. I didn't have any plans for the future. I didn't know what I was going to do when I got out. After Pearl Harbor, my future was decided for me.

I had a friend by the name of Carl Black who was a second lieutenant. Carl came by one day and said, "Let's go take the physical exam for the Air Force. They're dying for air crews." I said, "I don't think I want to. Besides, I wear glasses." He said, "Oh, come on, they give you three days off." So I went with Carl and took the physical. Carl is a good-looking, strapping guy, and had been an all-southern quarterback. He flunked the physical and I passed. I threw the glasses away, and never put them on again until I was 48 years old.

I had tried to learn to fly another time in Georgia at my own expense. I had a roommate that was nuts about flying, and I went along with him. I was petrified. I heard all this hangar talk about tailspins and I thought, "Oh, I'll never be able to survive that." A little-bitty lady was teaching me to fly, and it cost seven dollars an hour. Flying was a deep mystery to me. I could not understand the torque caused by that engine on takeoff. It was just a little-bitty airplane, a little two-cylinder. It sounded like a lawn mower. Finally, in desperation, she took me aside one day—she was about five feet tall—and said to me, "You're the dumbest son of a bitch I ever saw in my life, and you'll never learn to fly." She needed the money so my lessons continued, but that's how bad I was.

I went to flight school as a second lieutenant, which was a pretty nifty deal because I outranked the instructors. It was at Hicks Field in Fort Worth, which is a civilian school. Much to my surprise, I learned to fly. The instructor had four students, and two of us passed and two busted out. First I went to Randolph Air Force Base and then to Kelly Air Force Base. I graduated from Kelly in '42.

When I got out of flying school, Mom and Dad came to San Antonio to see me get my wings. A.A. was growing by then and they had an A.A. buddy there who owned a restaurant. Wherever they went, they had friends.

Next I got sent to a twin engine school. They assigned us according to temperament and size, and because I was pretty big, they decided I ought to be in the bombers. The little guys went to the fighters since they fit into them real nice. Usually they were feisty anyway. So they made them fighter pilots and I got sent to twin engine, an A-20, which was an attack bomber.

I was in Charlotte, North Carolina, when I got my orders to go overseas. I had to call Dad up and say, "Dad, I've got a car down here, and they've only given me a day and a half to get ready to leave. Can you come down or send somebody to get it?" So he called some A.A. guy who came down to Charlotte and picked up my car. I was already gone by the time he got there. I don't even know to this day who he sent, but somebody came down, picked up that car, and brought it back. That's how much A.A. had grown by then.

Twelve hours out of my school, I started to cross the south Atlantic as the pilot of an A-20. We were among the first combat crews ever to fly the South Atlantic. We went to Africa. Then the A-20 outfit was broken up, and I was assigned to a pilot pool.

I started again as a copilot in a B-24 outfit in a four-engine Liberator. We were flying out on anti-submarine patrol. We were covering the convoys out to sea. We'd go out as far as fifteen hundred miles. These were 11-hour, 13-hour, once in a while, 17-hour missions.

My outfit suffered a lot of losses. We lost about half the people. We were the third outfit, I understand, ever to get the Presidential Citation. First there was Torpedo Squadron 8, then the 19th Bomb Group, and then ours.

Because of the losses we suffered, I went from the newest copilot to flight commander of the lead flyers in six months. I had flown as a copilot with a pilot who became an operations officer for the squad room. When he advanced, I got his crew.

This squadron commander came to me one night and said, "One of the pilots in your outfit is having trouble. Ride with him and see if you can figure out what his problem is and help him. I need to fly a mission to get some time in, so I'll take your crew." So he took my crew out and they never came back. All my crew was dead. This was in '42 or '43. Later on, we were relieved by the Navy, and the whole outfit came home.

We came home about Thanksgiving of '43. We had developed a leak in one of the fuel tanks in Puerto Rico. The word was that we were going to have to stay there until they fixed the tank. It was one of the inboard tanks, with thousands of little bolts. So I figured it out and talked it over with my crew, and we figured that we could empty one of the fuel tanks on one side, and then fly on engine cross-feed into West Palm Beach, Florida, where they had a big depot. So we did. They just had a fit when we landed in the States. They couldn't believe that anybody would do that. So they grounded the airplane and started on the repairs.

I landed in the States with four hundred dollars. I rented a big Buick convertible, and, boy, I really cut a swath through Florida. I guess we were the first combat crew to ever come home in that area. The city was ours. I ran out of that four hundred bucks. I had to wire Dad to send me some more money. I had been sending him my pay to put in a savings account for when I got back, so I had a lot to play with. Oh, it was wild.

It took them three or four weeks to fix the fuel tank. Then they had to do it all over again because they changed the wrong fuel cell! All those thousands of screws, and they changed the wrong one. And all we were going to do with the old airplane was fly it up to Langley Field in Virginia and leave it there. Later on they were going to fly it out to Davis-Monthan Field in Tucson, which was the bone yard of all those old war-wearies. I guess that's where it ended up.

I was home for Christmas. For the first time my father let me drive his car. You talk about being grown up. I finally got to drive Dad's car. He finally realized that I had grown up. By this time, he was beginning to be a little proud of myself because I had been such a screw-up before. We were getting along well. It was working out good.

Susie was married to Ernie then, and we'd see her occasionally. They were doing pretty good, too and Ernie was kind of a commercial success. It was a nice Christmas.

My life was going along just fine. I was single. I got assigned to Clovis (NM) Army Air Base, which was a B-29 base. I was assistant base operations officer. By then I was drawing flying pay, and when I got down to Clovis I was a captain. I was really riding high. I wasn't looking ahead. I was just doing what I had to do right then.

Just before I went overseas I had a girlfriend who I was pretty content with. I had decided that I wouldn't get married until I came back, *if* I came back, because things were so uncertain. This girl lived in San Antonio. She was there when I got my wings, and she pinned my wings on me. My mother said something to me about that girl. You know, Mother was one of those people who seemed to have insight into people. She said, "That is a very unhappy lady." And it turned out she was right.

Mother sensed that she was just one of those people that never seems to find a place in life. Anyway, her letters got less and less frequent. I called her when I hit the States, and she was out dancing with some guy and kind of gave me the brush-off. I was hurt sore over that, and I decided, well, it isn't to be. Later on her sister called me and said this girl was just beside herself, crying and so forth. I told her sister, "I've cried all the tears I intend to over that lady. Thanks anyway."

Then I met Betty, my bride. I met her down there at Clovis at an Officer's Club dance. I was really taken. Betty's a very pretty lady, a knockout. That's what attracted me to her at first. We fell in love and got married out there on the base. I met her in early '44 and married her eight months later in October.

We went home to meet the family before we were married. We were getting pretty serious. Aside from being a beauty, Betty had a lot of deeper characteristics, and I liked that. We had good times together. We liked to drink and we liked to dance. Her father was an alcoholic at this point, but I didn't even know it. I never had seen the old guy sober. I thought he was just senile.

We hadn't talked about it at all. She didn't want me to know. She and I went back to Ohio so the folks could look her over. I wanted to be sure they got in on it this time. And they loved her. While we were there we all went to a meeting, and Betty discovered A.A. I wondered why she was so excited about it. She was so interested. She quizzed my parents at great length and really showed a deep interest in it. I was kind of surprised. She took home a copy of the Big Book. Later on I found out why.

Smitty and Betty's wedding in October of 1944.

Betty and Smitty at marriage.

She took the Big Book home for her dad because she dearly loved her father. He was a real sweet guy. He wasn't nearly as excited about it, but, later on, he and Bob D. from California, who is still alive, started A.A. in New Mexico.

I didn't find out about her dad's alcoholism until after we were married, when she wanted to borrow the car to take her father to a drying out place in Denver. That's when we had a little meeting and told everybody. We talked it over. She found a place through their family doctor because there was no A.A. there.

After we were married, I was ready to leave the service. They let people out of the service on a point basis. You got certain points for different things —being married, decorations, time in the service, and so on. I was the second highest guy on the base, and I thought, boy, I'm going to be the second one off of here. And I was.

Paul S., one of the early A.A.s, got me a job in Cleveland, Ohio, working for a tire dealer as service manager. We bought a little place in Bay Village. I stuck with that about a year.

I thought I could do better. I had saved my money while in the Air Force. My father had put it in the bank for me, paid the child support, and I still had several thousand dollars. There wasn't anything to spend it on in Africa where I had been stationed.

So we loaded up and sold our house. Dad had bought Betty and me a sofa from an estate sale. It was a beautiful, Victorian, silk-covered sofa for our little house in Bay Village. We were so glad to get it. Then Betty and I decided that what we needed was sectional furniture, which was the rage at the time. So I sawed that sofa in two, and we put a slipcover over each piece, and I made some makeshift legs. When my father and mother came up and saw that, I don't know how he did it, but Dad never said a word. I would have had a wild-eyed fit, but he handled it beautifully. There's his gorgeous sofa, and these two idiots had just taken a saw and cut it in two. It was absolutely horrible.

That year, '45-'46, we were pretty close with the folks. We were 40 miles from each other, so we did a lot of visiting. And when I worked in Cleveland, I'd seen them a lot. Every week the boss would rent a truck and send me down to Akron to pick up the tires he'd ordered. He had the wildest bunch working for him, and I was the only one that he'd trust to drive.

So I would drive as fast as I could, and I'd have time to have lunch with my mother. We had some wonderful visits, just the two of us.

I would see Susie sometimes, and Ernie. Ernie was a likeable guy, full of that Irish blarney. He had as much "B.S." as a Christmas turkey. He could also be very entertaining. He liked to put on a show.

But he would do some things that weren't even logical. For instance, every spring, just before he was going to start his driveway business, the first thing Ernie did was go down to the bank and borrow enough money to buy a brand new black Cadillac Fleetwood. He hadn't started working yet, but he borrowed enough money to trade his old one in and get a brand-new Cadillac. It was always a Fleetwood sedan and it was always black. He justified it as being a tool of his trade, but really and truly, it would scare the prospects to death. He was a funny guy.

Susie and I weren't close. We weren't feuding, we were just leading our own lives, I guess. Actually I think the relationship that I have with Susie has grown closer throughout the years. The older we get, the closer we get.

But then I decided that Betty and I were going back to New Mexico. Of course the folks were real disappointed with that. We sold the house. We went to Hobbs, New Mexico, where I was a partner in a garage and car storage place. It just didn't make any money. It was in a bad part of town. I finally sold out to my partner. I got out with a few dollars, but not much. I lost most of the capital I had saved when I was overseas.

14

TREADMILL

I felt pretty bad about the business failure. This was my first venture on my own, it was going down the tube, and there didn't seem to be anything that I could do about it. I shouldn't have bought it in the first place.

But we didn't leave Hobbs. I decided that I wanted to learn something about the oil business, so I got a job as a roughneck on a drilling rig. The company was drilling some 7,000-foot wells down in Eunice, New Mexico. I started right at the very bottom.

I got a job later on with a service company that had a unique angle—they could work on the wells with the pressure still on. I knew it was a very unusual trade that could be very lucrative. There were very few people who knew anything about it. I worked for them for five years, and I used what they taught me later on in my own company.

That same company found out that I had been a pilot. They had a small aviation department going and they wanted somebody who could fly. So they brought me into Dallas, and I became the company pilot. I had some GI Bill money coming, so I took instrument training to get the corporation's insurance down, and I finally got my airline transport license. This is the same license that the captain on an airliner has, and, as far as I know, it's the highest aeronautical rating that you can get.

I flew until Betty got fed up with my being gone all the time. My boss had a daughter at Wellesley, so I'd fly him up there to see his daughter and then I would either stay in Boston or take the airplane down to Teterboro, New Jersey, and call on the export trade in New York City. Then I'd see Broadway plays at night. This went on for two or three years. Betty was home, wiping noses and paying the mortgage. We had three kids, and she was trying to do it all while I was off hunting in Mexico or on a cruise on the St. Lawrence or in New York City, calling on the export trade and seeing Broadway plays.

I could see there was no future in the job. You hit 40, and the boss begins to wonder whether or not you're going to have a heart attack. You're the only one up there in the cockpit. I was the whole aviation department, and my boss expected me to fly the weather just like the airliners. It's pretty tough for one guy to handle the flying and the radio and all the instruments. There wasn't any auto pilot. I could see there wasn't much future in that. I told Betty I'd fly for so much longer and then I'd quit, and there would surely be something else we could do.

While I was still flying, we lived in a very modest home in Irving, Texas. I wasn't even there when they closed the deal on that house. I was off flying someplace, so Betty had to do all that. Mother and Father came down there to visit in '49, for a week or two. Scott, our oldest son, was just a toddler. He was out there in a mud puddle splashing away when they arrived, and my mother was so tickled. Anyway, she got a cold and a kind of flu. Even though my father was there, I got hold of a friend who was also a doctor, and he came over. He wasn't a very good doctor, I figured out later, and he was an alcoholic himself. But he gave Mom a little medicine. It was hot and we didn't have any air conditioning. With all that, Mother decided that she wanted to go home.

And so they started home. Actually, mom and dad had just started to fly. Before that they never would fly. But in '49, when my folks came down to visit us, my boss said, "Take them up in the airplane and show them the big flood that we had." And so they agreed to go up with me. I guess they figured, "Heck, we'll all go out together." They weren't at all uneasy, and after that they started flying.

Dad got mom on an airplane to go home, and they started having all kinds of trouble. She got seriously ill in Chicago before he finally got her back to Akron. By then he was a dying man himself, and he knew it. His cancer had already progressed for four or five years. She died first—in the hospital in Akron. When my father called me, he was absolutely shattered.

I was totally surprised when she died. I knew that for some reason she had a very strong desire to go home, but I had thought it was just due to the terribly hot weather.

I was at home when he called. It was during the early evening. I was, of course, terribly shocked and worried for him. He was so upset and so broken up. I went back; Betty didn't go. She stayed with the kids.

At the time Mom died, she was losing her eyesight. That was the biggest problem. She had had a cataract operation performed by George Ferguson, a dear friend of my parents. He was the most prominent eye doctor in Akron. In those days, after one of those operations you had to lie perfectly still for weeks. And then her eye became infected.

She lost the sight in that eye, and the other one had a cataract also. Her sight became progressively dimmer. She got to the point where she could recognize that there was someone sitting over there, but she wouldn't know who it was until she heard their voice. She wouldn't have the other eye operated on because she could still see some. She just kept going. It didn't seem to daunt her spirit. She still sent Christmas cards, only she started writing them in September.

One time when I was home I said to her, "Mom, you've got such a strong faith, didn't you ever pray that you'd be able to see?" She said, "Oh, yes, often." I said, "Well, how come nothing happened?" And she said, "Well, I don't know; maybe my faith wasn't strong enough."

I never realized how much my mother contributed to A.A. until she died. She was so subtle and so undemanding and so unpretentious that it just slipped by me how great she was. But then when she died a year before my father, I realized how totally he relied upon her, what a rock she was. He was generally considered to be the rock behind A.A., but she was the rock behind the rock.

I had more of a warning with Dad's death because he was in and out of the hospital so many times. In fact, one time we thought he was going, so I came up. You know, a cancer patient rallies from time to time, but they don't ever rally quite as high. Each rally is a little bit weaker. So, his death was expected.

Anne near her death in 1949.
At the time her vision was almost gone.

The last trip that we went on—Betty, Dr. Bob, and I—was immediately after the A.A. First International in 1950. He had the car of his dreams —a Buick Roadmaster convertible. The funny part was that the older he got, the faster he drove.

He was terminally ill; he knew it and we knew it. He was barely able to talk for just a few minutes at that First International. We heard that wonderful talk where he said it all boils down to love and service, and to "keep it simple."

Then Betty and I drove him back to his beloved Vermont for the last time in his convertible. We had some wonderful, sharing, poignant memories, when we'd sit on the bed at night and talk to each other. When he got to St. Johnsbury, most of his old cronies had already died or moved away. There really was just the one elderly widow he was close friends with. So it was kind of a sad time for him too, because he knew he would never be back. We drove him back through the Finger Lakes of New York and back to Akron. Betty and I left immediately. I never saw him alive again.

My dad went through a lot of suffering. Trying to postpone death with frequent surgery made the quality of his life pretty bad. He was already a lonesome man since my mother had died the year before. I realized then what a strength she had been for him. It came to me forcibly how important she had always been for him.

I didn't know how big A.A. had become until that First International. Then at Dad's funeral, it became very apparent. Bill came down, of course, and a friend of his—Hank. They were very much take-charge people, and they had the funeral pretty well organized.

Susie and I had our input. We wanted Dr. Tunks to do it. The number of people who turned up from all walks of life, all genuinely bereaved, was very, very impressive. I think I was 32 at the time, but I began to realize the impact Dr. Bob and Bill W. were having. People came in from all over the country, all sorts of people, from the poorest to the wealthiest. I began to realize what a tremendous thing A.A. was becoming.

I don't know if you've experienced this or not, but when you lose your last parent, there is a feeling that comes over you when you realize that there is nobody left in this world that has that special love that your parents have. Nobody. You have a real sense of loss. You're strictly on your own.

147

We were living in Irving at the time. We lived on a street with a lot of young married people and a lot of people involved in the aviation industry. It was a real partying neighborhood. Wow, the parties they threw. We used to actually try to avoid them, because there were so many of them. I was gone a lot and then I'd come home to all these parties.

Then I went into business for myself and was gone again most of the time trying to get the thing started. The name of the corporation was Pressure Services, Incorporated. I had two partners, and we did really well. We did two separate, distinct things. We were manufacturing our own oil-field tools and selling them, and one fellow was in charge of that. The other guy and I went out and did the pressure work. We worked over oil wells with the pressure still on.

Some wells you can't kill and get them quiet. The only way you can work on them is with the pressure still on. It's a hard, dangerous job. The gas pressure is trying to force all that stuff out of the ground. It ended up that I was doing all the pressure work. One of my partners had broken his neck doing it, and the other one had broken his back. It was a dangerous thing, but it paid well.

Soon after we started I worked over a helium well under pressure for the Bureau of Mines in New Mexico. I was up there 153 days on that job, so I wasn't home very much. But we made a lot of money quickly. By then I only had one partner in the corporation, and later I sold out to him. With the money that I got from the sale, I came up here to Nocona and bought some old stripper production wells in the north part of town. Stripper production refers to wells that just produce marginally. The wells get their name from just barely stripping the oil out of the ground. There's a shallow field just north of here that a small independent producer can handle. And we've been at that type of business ever since. I came here in October of '55, and Betty and the kids came in January of '56. We never got rich, but we've been comfortable.

148

15
TAKING STEPS

In the years after Mother and Dad died, we went on with our lives. You know how it is. We were having a good time. We were raising kids. We were doing the parent stuff. Betty was into the PTA. She was teaching Sunday school. I was a deacon and an elder in the church; not very deep, but I was there. We were doing the family bit that most people get into. We were getting along pretty good. There were no health problems and no kid problems.

We thought we were accomplishing something—raising a family and trying to be a part of the community. I served on the school board and seven years on the hospital board. Later on I served four years on the city council. We tried to be part of the community.

We were doing real well financially. We built our own home. The cars were paid for and the kids' college was under control. And it began to dawn on me, "Is this all there is?"

That's when I began to give it a little more thought. That's, I guess, the first time that it had really occurred to me that life wasn't all a pursuit of material things. I felt something was lacking.

Then came 1965. It was a terrible year. I had a lung collapse twice. And at age 44, nineteen years after our last child was born, Betty had twins, born premature. One of them, the little girl, died at birth. Our son, Todd, the twin that lived, is a joy to us. He's going to school to be an optometrist now.

But 1965 was a traumatic year for us. Betty was in a dangerous pregnancy and I had to prop myself up on a pillow every night just to breathe in and out. I was a heavy smoker and couldn't quit. Then one of the babies died. It was bad. But even then I thought that we were perfectly able to handle it. I thought I was sufficient for all things. I felt absolutely able to handle it.

We liked to drink and we liked to party. You know, when Betty first started drinking, she would drink two drinks and be deadly sick for a couple of days. It was absolute poison to her. But with my encouragement, she persevered. We never thought of alcoholism as anything we had to worry about. We never thought of it. I don't think anybody had given much thought to a genetic predisposition to it, not even the medical profession.

Our drinking got to be pretty heavy. Once when we lived up near Cleveland, in Bay Village, we quit for a year. We only started again when this old friend of ours from Irving came up. We bought some bourbon to celebrate him coming, and we started drinking again. Later on, incidentally, he became a member of A.A.

We never had a big liquor cabinet—just a busy one. It was insidious. I was an enthusiastic drinker, but I never drank on the job and I never missed a day of work. And I never wanted to drink in the morning. Maybe it was because I had such a strong work ethic. I don't know.

After the older kids were grown Betty wasn't working, so she had plenty of time on her hands. And she started drinking in the daytime. I never asked Betty to quit drinking. I just asked her to quit getting so damn drunk. I was kind of enjoying her company, as far as the partying went.

But then the fun began to wear thin, and you could see the seamy side of it coming on. There wasn't any joy anymore. The booze used to tear up my stomach. I had my secret supply that was hidden from Betty, and she had her secret supply that was hidden from me. And she would water down the bottles in our common bar.

It started to be a problem for me when she would be passed out at night, and when I had to caution her and threaten her when we were going to a party. I'd say, "Two drinks, and don't you dare take any more." When she would take two drinks and be plastered, I realized that she had been priming the pump before the party. At some point, the invisible line was crossed.

It got to the point where we were having blackouts and hangovers together and hiding our booze from each other. It was absolute despair. But it didn't dawn on us that Betty needed treatment. In the first place, we didn't have any insurance. In the second place, we didn't recognize alcoholism in our home, believe it or not.

I never said, "Hey, you need to go to A.A.," or "You need treatment." And I didn't say, "Stop drinking." I said, "I want you to quit getting so damn drunk," because I wanted to party still. I had a little different idea yet. I could see some of the fun was going out of it. But then, you're still hanging on because that's the only way you know. The drinking and the partying is the only way you know.

We didn't want to change our lifestyles. We didn't like what was happening, but we had become accustomed to it. It's the change that we feared. We looked around, and the people that never took a drink weren't very damn interesting to us. We certainly wouldn't have them as friends. They were just so dull. So it was scary. You know, what do you do on Saturday night? What do people do with their evenings? Do they all sit around and sing hymns? "Is there life after sobriety?" is the way I've heard it expressed. That's a big fear.

So two or three times when I walked in on Betty sitting in the living room playing records of Dr. Bob's talks and reading the Big Book, I wasn't real interested. I'd say, "Having a little meeting of your own, dear?" and that would be it. I'd pass right by on my way to the bar.

To paraphrase Kahlil Gibran, alcoholism entered our house as a guest, then became the host, and then the master. Betty was trying desperately to quit; I wasn't done partying yet. I could see this was giving her a bad time, but I didn't really know how bad because I was working all day.

It finally got so bad that Betty's mother said to me one time, "Why don't you ask her for a divorce? That will shock her." So I broached the subject to her, but it didn't shock her as much as I thought it ought to. What I didn't realize is that the disease had become her number-one priority, and the family had moved down the line somewhere. By the nature of the disease, it just has to happen that way.

Betty was the one, finally. She did it herself. She came to me and said, "Will you go with me?" I said, "No, as far as the program goes, you stand alone. This is something you've got to do for yourself. If you think you have to go, go ahead."

She had tried every way in the world, but she couldn't stop. Finally, March 13 of '79, a local guy called up and said, "Betty, we're starting a group here for people that have a problem like you and me, will you come?" She said, "Wonder how he knew?" Hell, they had never seen each other sober. So she went, and she took off running. She's been sober ever since.

I began to see the change in her. That's when I really got interested, because the thought had already dawned on me that there had to be something more in life than just this accumulation of material things and so forth. I didn't know what it was, but I saw something new in her.

I began wanting some of the things she was getting. I can't remember any details; my mind doesn't work that way. But I began showing some interest in the changes. Shortly thereafter, I began driving 40 miles to my own Twelve-Step meetings.

I didn't mind joining the auxiliary program. I felt like I was the rock that was holding the family together anyway. Possibly a few character defects. Nothing serious. I had just enough knowledge about alcoholism to be absolutely dangerous. Then I walk into the meeting, and I'm the only man. There's 20 or 30 ladies sitting there. I like to tell people that I had "mixed emotions." It was like when your teenaged daughter comes in at four in the morning with a Gideon Bible under her arm—that's mixed emotions.

A few weeks ago I ran into some of the ladies from that group, and we started talking about the first meeting I went to. They told me something that came as a complete surprise to me. They said after hearing what I had to say that night, "We doubted you'd ever make it." Here I went there thinking I was just about perfect, and they were privately concluding I was just about terminal. Fortunately for me, the people that were there were serious about the program and I did get help.

Most people come in with the idea that they're going to "get the sucker that's drinking." That's their main purpose. The second thing they want is to sit down and tell you about that dirty S.O.B. That's part of recovery, and you're going to have to listen to it. But one time's plenty. You can't let 'em wallow in their anger and resentment. And they're shocked to find out that they don't keep talking about that so-called "sucker." They talk about getting themselves well. I still love to go to that group because I feel like I'm coming home, you know.

At first I didn't really know why I was there. Then it was explained to me that it was a program of recovery for the family, and that—whether they realized it or not—the family had been seriously affected by the disease.

I didn't think I had been affected. Not at first. When I first heard about the problems of children of alcoholics I thought, "Boy, what a cop out, blame it all on the alcoholic." And, "Gee, this is a crock." It didn't dawn on me for quite a while that yes, alcoholism affects me. Yes, I've been affected. Yes, I was still affected.

It's hard to think of specific examples, because I don't have that kind of memory. But I began to realize that the life pattern that I had was not completely whole. I learned that when you are raised in an alcoholic home, there are some gaps in your development as a totally complete person: mentally, spiritually, psychologically, socially, whatever categories you choose to use. In thinking about that, I began to realize there were some real gaps. Also, I had some very false goals. I thought material things were going to make me happy.

I think I totally missed how to obtain happiness. It totally escaped me. I had confused pleasure and happiness. You know, pleasure comes when you buy a new car: It gives you an awful lot of pleasure through the third payment, but that's it. Happiness is something that's permanent. And I had been seeking happiness through pleasure all my life by satisfying the urge for material things. My personality was self-centered and materially oriented. There was nothing spiritual. That was the big gap in me.

I was lucky that I was put in a position where I could change. I was lucky to have a partner that sought help because, frankly, I never would have gotten there by myself. I know that. I would have gone on indefinitely like I was, because I knew how to do it real well. I wasn't in what you would call a crisis.

Gradually, I allowed myself to start the inspection and the examination of the effect of being raised in an alcoholic home. It allowed me to start opening those doors in my memory, which is a difficult thing for anybody to do, because we tend to shut out the bad and remember the good.

The Twelve Steps showed me a better way of life, one that I wasn't smart enough to figure out for myself. I found out it all boils down to love and service, like old Doc said at that First International right before he died. I couldn't know it then. I had to learn it. It was a slow, slow, gradual process.

I kept on drinking for about eight weeks after Betty quit. But I told her, "If having this stuff around bothers you, let me know." Well, the hot water heater exploded one day when I was out of town, and she moved the booze out to the garage where it wouldn't be so available in a crisis. And one night I came in and drank a six-pack of beer and got kind of silly, and she told me it bothered her so I said, "Okay, let's just get rid of it." I don't drink anymore.

I have a real strong A.A. friend who runs an alcohol treatment center in Pennsylvania. He worked me over one time and was trying to convince me that I am an alcoholic even though I quit drinking shortly after Betty did. He really shook me up for a long time. I thought, "Well, hell, am I flying under the wrong colors?" I wouldn't intentionally do that, at least I don't think I would. I had to think about that a long, long time, and I finally decided that I am in the program that I ought to be in. I don't think I am an alcoholic. But he really instilled some doubts in my mind that I had to work out myself.

With both Betty and I sober, I've had to learn some new things. I'm learning that two people need space—individual space. There are times in our relationship now where I have to get in my car and drive off—actually drive off—to avoid a conflict about something that is probably inconsequential anyway.

Another thing I've learned is that you've got to give and you've got to learn to accept. That was tough for me. Giving was not as tough for me as learning how to accept gracefully. I'm still learning, but I'm a lot better.

Another thing I've gained is self-esteem. I've got to say I've never had the low self-esteem that most alcoholics have. I had some doubts, but I've always been able to handle it by going to the material things, which was my way of coping. People like me, if they don't make a change, they're comfortable functioning like they are. I hate to use the word "dysfunctional," but I know how to function in a situation that doesn't function very well. I know how to do that beautifully, as that's my natural tendency. You do what you know how to do.

I've read that working a Twelve-Step program makes us the persons we were meant to be. Well, it's not easy. Being Doctor Bob's son was no help. I had to work on this like everybody else. I didn't have any special insights. I made all the mistakes. I went immediately from the first three Steps to the Twelfth Step. I skipped all those in between. I became a savior of the world. I don't know how many lives I personally screwed up not knowing what I was talking about.

I had a heck of a time doing the Fourth Step, because I didn't want to do the Fifth Step. I didn't like the idea of telling all my weaknesses and so forth to another person. I already knew 'em and so did God, but it was the idea of letting the barrier down to talk to another person that was a real hang-up with me. Finally, I did it. It took me a year.

I had gutted up and decided I was going to do it because I was as ready as I was going to be. I decided on the person, and I made three runs at him before I finally caught up with him. Each time I had to go back and rethink it, and get a little bit more of a handle on it. But the third time, when I finally caught up with him and was able to do it, I was probably a lot better prepared than I was when I first went out looking for him.

Like I said, I came into the program thinking I was just about perfect. A few minor character defects. Nothing serious. But I learned I had an awful lot of defects—and they aren't minor! I have to continually work on them. I was self-centered, extremely selfish, opinionated, and closed-minded about a lot of things. I was very quick to anger, and held resentments for a long, long time. I was verbally abusive to my wife and children. And these were all things I had to face up to.

You spend a lot of time and effort building up a facade. And now you're called on to totally change that. I think what enables you to do it is that you find something so much better. But you know, you don't get it instantly. The change is not going to be overnight or you couldn't handle it. You're allowed to progress at your own speed. There are no term papers. It is not a test.

The Sixth and Seventh Steps are not as easy as you think, because there are a lot of defects of character that are delightful, that you revel in. Those are ones you don't want to be relieved from. Hell, you're enjoying 'em. So it takes a real desire to change. You can only do it if you see something better that you're trying to get to.

In Steps Eight and Nine, I began to make amends. I had to make amends to a guy who I thought the only reason the son of a bitch was on this earth was to aggravate me. I had to gut up and make amends to that guy, and you know what? He didn't accept 'em. This happens. But I told him at the time, "You don't have to accept it, but I've got to give it." When it was over I felt relieved, but he still disliked me heartily. He doesn't even speak to me. But I'm free of it, that's the beauty of the amends. You start getting freedom.

The last two Steps—well, there you're getting into the spirituality. I used to have a working relationship with God that was the panic-button type. When I got into trouble, I prayed for help. When I was a young kid, some old gentleman who was a missionary in Africa came and talked to us and gave us an emergency way to pray—"Oh, Lord Jesus, save me." Do it three times, and tell Him what the problem is and it will be solved. I had used that many times in an emergency and it had worked. It really worked. So I had that kind of faith.

I began to understand that there's a difference between spirituality and religion. Spirituality presented God to me in a light that I could accept and understand and want. And I learned the power of prayer. I don't think the purpose of prayer is to ask for anything. I think the purpose of prayer is to surrender.

After a while, you get to see the power of spirituality. I see thousands of people in my travels. As I go through the country, I see thousands of people who are absolute miracles. Somehow a Higher Power has intervened in their lives and changed a total wreck into a likeable, lovable human being who is trying to be of service. It's wonderful.

Working a Twelve-Step program has brought me closer to my mother and father, but in a different way. The lesson that they were able to teach, by example, really dawned on me when I started to give my own recovery serious thought. Initially, I think I had the same concept of humility that most people have. It's something to be avoided. It's degrading. It's demeaning. But that's not what it really means. I found out that it means to put yourself in a position where you can be taught something. That is the paradox.

Another thing I learned is when you are truly trying to be helpful and of service, you can talk to anybody. The economic strata and other barriers disappear. You are at ease with people. You're not there to be impressed, and you're not there to impress anybody. You're there to help. I've had to learn to be a listener, too.

Love and service, that's it, just like old Doc said. I had to learn how to love. I love to talk about that. You know, my father had problems with love. He said in one of his talks that he wasn't antagonistic toward his fellow man, but, "To love him," he said, "I just couldn't do it; I just couldn't do it." But he learned to love.

My dad was sober 15 years. In five of those years he was ill. In the other 10, he personally treated more than 5,000 people for alcoholism—medically —at no charge. Of course, back then we were interested in how we were going to get along financially, so we'd ask him every day: How'd you do today? He'd say he had three operations. And he'd say, "Two for the lord and one for R.H." (his first two initials). He operated on a lot of charity patients. He learned to love his fellow man.

I thought I was a very shallow person, because I didn't seem to be able to love my fellow man. I could see a deeper love in other people than I seemed to be able to have. I read a book that kind of set me on the right track on that one. It said love is a learned phenomenon, you're not born with it. And here's the catch, I think, for us—you have to be willing to accept love, which I could never do.

All of this was taught to me slowly. I had a sponsor who interested me in, and forced me into, the service end of it. I learned then that everybody in the program is not perfect. I learned they don't have to be perfect for you to love 'em or even like 'em. Because when you start culling your friends, accepting only the perfect ones, you're not going to have any friends. I used to cull my friends, and if I found the slightest imperfection, I would think I had to discard them. But now I seem to be able to accept them like they are, warts and all, and present myself to other people, warts and all. And, boy, you can sure have a lot more friends that way.

When it comes to people in Twelve-Step programs, Betty's dad, Pete A., said it the best I've ever heard anybody say it. "It seems as though when we have come through Steps One, Two, and Three, we have crawled away from the living dead, and the gates of the promised land are swung wide for us. And without exploring the land, we pick the first two-room shack we can find and settle down, not having the energy or the wish to explore further, where the finer sites are, where the great reaches and inspiring vistas wait for us. On and on the land is more fertile and beautiful. But we complacently accept the least we can have and proceed with our knitting." We think "I got in, didn't I?"

This is true for so many people. They settle for the first place they land in the program. And there is so much more if they will make the effort to actually work it. The program is continual. It will grow with you, if you just keep going. That's been an inspiration to me to keep doing what I'm doing. A lot of times I think, "Gee whiz, I'm tired of doing all these things." But I keep going and growing because there are better places to be.

I've finally got to where I can see where my mother and father were so many years ago. Even if Dad and Bill had started A.A. earlier, when I was much younger instead of in my late teens as it was, I don't think I would have learned anything from it. I had to do a lot of my own experiments, and forge my own little tunnel without the benefit of Dad's influence.

He never tried to discuss any Twelve-Step wisdom with me. If he had, I probably would have gone my own way anyway because I'm kind of self-sufficient. That's my way of handling things. I certainly don't blame my father.

There are some things he tried to teach me that didn't dawn on me until I started working my own Twelve-Step program. I remember reflecting back and wondering, "Well, why did he do that?" Now I know why. While he was doing it, I thought, What a crock. This is the pits. Why is he dragging us around to all these churches? But now I can reflect on things he did, and I can see he was trying to give me something. Only I couldn't take it. Recovery is not something that can be given. I had to get to the point where I was looking for it. It took me 40 years.

We're lucky in my family. Neither Betty nor I was an active alcoholic when the first three children grew up, so they weren't affected. None of our kids are alcoholics, although I'm sure they had their moments and experimented. For example, I had bought Betty a brand-new Buick, and one night our oldest son took it out and got drunk and ran into a neighbor's oak tree. I got him up the next morning and made him, with a terrible hangover, go tell the guy that he did it. I don't think he even drinks now. He married a woman whose family doesn't—it's just not a part of their lives at all.

The two girls have maybe an occasional cocktail, maybe nothing. They both like health food stuff. So far the youngest son, who was there for our drinking, is one of those people who respects his body, always watches his diet, does karate, that kind of stuff. He doesn't appear to have been affected.

I know we passed on some things that we didn't want to pass on to them. We did it because we didn't know any better. With the first three children I had the absolute necessity to be totally in control. I was pretty stern. We had a lot of fun, but whatever I said was the law. There weren't many arguments. I just didn't allow it.

We used to get into some awful battles with the oldest. As a teenager, she stood up and slugged it out toe to toe with us. She was a strong individual, and later on this caused her some problems. We didn't know any better. We just didn't know. We've always been able to talk the talk. Well, now we're being forced to walk the walk. Sometimes we don't do it very well. We've got one kid who's got a bachelor's degree, and two of my children, a boy and a girl, have master's degrees. The other one's talking about being a doctor of optometry.

I've finally learned some of the stuff that my father went through 50 years ago. Now the question is, can I share it with my kids? I don't know. I'm much more open now. But you don't want to just bore them. I don't think you can pass on everything because, frankly, they have to learn it themselves. But you can pass on this program by example. And someday, if they are ready for it, they'll be able to use it.

The other day my youngest daughter came in with a new book on codependency. She got it from an entirely different angle, this concept of codependency. She doesn't relate it to alcoholism. She relates it to the relationship she has with her husband. Neither of them is alcoholic, but her book is about how to live. That's one thing I think about Twelve-Step programs—they're a formula for living that you can understand and that you can work. I heard recently that there are something like 200 different Twelve-Step programs today. Can you believe it? It just shows how the Twelve Steps can help with any problems people run into in life.

The story of A.A. shouldn't be sanitized. It was developed by people stuck in all kinds of trouble, but they still proceeded toward higher values. Look at what was going on with me and with Susie at that time. But the program was being developed, and it has saved millions of lives. It works, and it works for imperfect people living imperfect lives because it came out of imperfect people living imperfect lives. They didn't levitate; they struggled.

159

Betty and Smitty in 1988. "We've always been able to talk the talk. Well, now we're being forced to walk the walk."

There were dues that were paid for this program. I finally reached the point where I can accept it. I have a lot of failings that I continually have to work on. I still don't do it perfectly or even very well, but at least I make the effort.

I had a heart attack in 1988. It scared me. Now I'm the mayor of our town, and I look at it as a way to give some things back. I've got a lot of living left to do, and I intend to do it.

I've also got this full-sized Greyhound bus that I bought and turned into a motor home. It's real luxurious. It has a bathroom and a shower. Betty wanted a tub, so I put one of those in, too. The master bedroom has a queen-size bed. I did all the work on it myself. The kitchen is real nice. It's almost finished. When it is, I'm gonna' hit the road.

You may write to Sue or Bob at the following address:
c/o Parkside Publishing Corporation
205 West Touhy Avenue
Park Ridge, Illinois 60068